13 SECONDS

13 SECONDS

A Look Back at the Kent State Shootings

Philip Caputo

CHAMBERLAIN BROS.

A MEMBER OF PENGUIN GROUP (USA) INC.

NEW YORK

2005

CHAMBERLAIN BROS.
Published by the Penguin Group
Penguin Group (USA) Inc., 375 Hudson Street,
New York, New York 10014, USA
Penguin Group (Canada), 10 Alcorn Avenue,
Toronto, Ontario M4V 3B2, Canada (a division of Pearson Penguin Canada Inc.)
Penguin Books Ltd, 80 Strand, London WC2R 0RL, England
Penguin Ireland, 25 St Stephen's Green,
Dublin 2, Ireland (a division of Penguin Books Ltd)
Penguin Group (Australia), 250 Camberwell Road,
Camberwell, Victoria 3124, Australia
(a division of Pearson Australia Group Pty Ltd)
Penguin Books India Pvt Ltd, 11 Community Centre,
Panchsheel Park, New Delhi—110 017, India
Penguin Group (NZ), Cnr Airborne and Rosedale Roads, Albany,
Auckland 1310, New Zealand
(a division of Pearson New Zealand Ltd)
Penguin Books (South Africa) (Pty) Ltd, 24 Sturdee Avenue, Rosebank,
Johannesburg 2196, South Africa

Penguin Books Ltd, Registered Offices: 80 Strand,
London WC2R 0RL, England

Letters, poems, and chronologies courtesy of Kent State University Libraries and
Media Services, Department of Special Collections and Archives,
http://speccoll.library.kent.edu/4may70/exhibit/chronology/index.html.
Used with permission.

An application has been submitted to register this book with the Library of Congress.

ISBN 1-59609-080-4

Printed in the United States of America
1 3 5 7 9 10 8 6 4 2

Book design by Joseph Rutt

While the author has made every effort to provide accurate telephone numbers and Inter-
net addresses at the time of publication, neither the publisher nor the author assumes any
responsibility for errors, or for changes that occur after publication. Further, the publisher
does not have any control over and does not assume any responsibility for author or third-
party Web sites or their content.

For my granddaughter, Livia Marie Caputo,
and my niece, Lindsay Peyton Ellis

Acknowledgments

With thanks to the Kent State University May 4 Resource Center.

Chapter 1

Driving I-76 through Akron, in the heart of the heart of the Midwestern rust belt, I am trying to remember which route I followed from the Cleveland airport nearly thirty-five years ago. It isn't important, but I want to withdraw even the small details from the vault of memory. I don't recall taking an interstate—I'm fairly sure there was none linking Cleveland and Akron back then. My recollection is of a two-lane blacktop bending through the Ohio countryside, past barns and farmhouses and plowed fields and dogwoods sprouting white blossoms in the soft light of early May.

The exit signs read: KENT—RAVENNA—KENT STATE UNIVERSITY. I turn off to drive north on Route 43, which could be the highway I took in 1970, but from the opposite direction. There are no dogwood blossoms today. It's late October, the trees blaze like fireworks. The countryside has changed, is indeed no longer countryside. Most of the barns and farmhouses have been razed, subdivisions grow where corn once did; fast-food franchises, car dealerships, shopping malls, muffler and brake shops sprawl across former pastures. For all practical purposes, once-rural Kent now belongs to exurbia, the "urb" being gritty Akron, ten or fifteen miles away.

The car radio crackles with news of the 2004 presidential race. The campaign is in its final, frantic week, and the two candidates are storming Ohio—a "key battleground state" in media shorthand. President Bush will be speaking in the Cleveland suburbs and in Dayton, challenger John Kerry is in Toledo before heading on to a rally that will be led off by The Boss, Bruce Springsteen. I cannot help but think of the news that Monday in May, the bulletins that interrupted regular programming. That was how I'd heard about it, on the car radio, and I remember stepping on the gas, racing down the two-lane blacktop toward the university, where the Ohio National Guard had opened fire on a crowd of student demonstrators.

Like the countryside, the campus has changed dramatically. It is bigger, with more buildings and more roads. Blue-and-white signs direct visitors to the North, South, and East campuses. I am not sure which one to go to, until I spot a sign that says "May 4 Memorial," with an arrow pointing to the right. There is another farther on, then no more and I am soon lost. Parking near the Ice Arena, a low, almost windowless building of pale brown brick, I check a campus map in a glassed-in box on the corner. The key alongside the map informs me that the memorial is near Taylor and Prentice halls, some distance from the Ice Arena.

Taylor Hall—that flips a switch in my memory. I return to my car, stepping over the words "Celebrate Responsibly" painted on the sidewalk at regular intervals. I assume this is an admonition not to get drunk and rowdy after a hockey game, but it may mean something else entirely.

At any rate, the students appear admirably sober and responsible on this fair autumn morning as they stroll to and from their classes in baggy clothes, backpacks stuffed full of books. A security guard directs me to a visitors' parking lot. I get out, walk up a dirt path, and see Taylor Hall, an imposing concrete structure atop a hill. It was one of the newer buildings on campus in 1970; now it has attained venerable status, though its architecture—nondescript, twentieth-century modern—belies that description. It still looks new.

The hill slopes down in a sweep of green to a green field. That must be the practice field where the guardsmen knelt and fired with their World War II M-1 rifles. It is quite peaceful today, empty, banal. Below, I spot what appears to be a marker, walk to it, and discover that it's merely a piece of sculpture. Somewhat frustrated, I climb back up and ask a student, "Is the memorial around here?"

"Right over there," he says, pointing at a clump of trees.

It is unobtrusive to say the least, almost covert, hidden under a grove of oaks and maples: a marble tablet set in the ground near some marble slabs that, I guess, serve as benches.

The sole decorations are a few artificial flowers bound with pink and purple ribbon, a foil pinwheel that turns lazily in the breeze, the blades silver on one side, painted with the stars and stripes on the other. Its modesty seems deliberate, as if it commemorated a dark secret, like the gravestone of a relative who shamed the family. The tablet is covered with dead leaves, which I brush off to read the chiseled legend:

IN LOVING MEMORY
Allison Krause
Jeffrey Miller
Sandra Scheuer
William Schroeder

RESPECTFULLY REMEMBERED
Alan Canfora
John Cleary
Thomas Grace
Dean Kahler
Joseph Lewis
Donald Mackenzie
James Russell
Robby Stamps
Douglas Wrentmore

For all its uninspiring nature, it is a kind of war memorial, honoring the casualties of the day when the Vietnam War came home.

There are four other markers in the Prentice Hall parking lot near Taylor Hall, one each for the dead. I have a vivid memory of the parking lot, stained with their blood and the blood of the wounded, and I carry it with me as I leave the campus and drive through Kent, its business district, like most in American small towns, half ghost town, half museum, vitality sucked out by Wal-Marts and Home Depots, then head down Route 43 for the interstate, my brain reeling back in time while the car rolls forward.

In the spring of 1970, I was a twenty-eight-year-old general assignment reporter for the *Chicago Tribune*, three years out of the United States Marine Corps, with which I had served a tour of duty in Vietnam. In March, the paper had sent me to cover a student protest at the University of Illinois in downstate Champaign-Urbana. Demonstrations for black civil rights or against the war had become fixtures of American college life, replacing panty raids and pep rallies. Compared with those that had occurred in previous years at such incubators of antiwar rage as the University of Chicago, the University of Wisconsin, Columbia, and Berkeley, the one at U. of I. was fairly tame. A leftist student group calling itself the Radical Union staged a sit-in to

protest military recruitment on campus as well as recruitment by corporations with ties to the defense industry,
most notably General Electric. The demonstrators were also
expressing their disagreement with a decision by university
authorities to bar William Kunstler, the celebrity lawyer
who'd defended the Chicago Seven after the Democratic
convention riots in Chicago in 1968, from speaking at the
school.

On March 2, some eight hundred students ranged
through the campus, breaking windows in the armory and
the electrical engineering building, and then proceeded to
the business district of Champaign-Urbana, where more
windows were sacrificed to the cause. On a scale of one to
ten, damages rated about a three: $15,000 to $20,000.
Richard Ogilvie, governor of Illinois at the time, ordered
National Guard units on standby, and state police were
called in to assist the campus and city law enforcement de-
partments. A curfew was imposed.

Over the next two days, two to three hundred members
of the Radical Union and their followers occupied the third
and fourth floors of the student union building, where the
corporate recruiters had been extolling the virtues of their
companies to prospective graduates. National Guardsmen
were then summoned to the campus, while state troopers
cleared the floors of protestors, who marched out peaceably
to chants of "Power to the people," though a few took a mo-

ment to kick the doors of the rooms in which the recruiters had barricaded themselves. There was a nighttime demonstration at the armory and in front of the home of David Henry, the university president. Police arrested one hundred forty-seven people, all but two for curfew violations, and university chancellor Jack Pelatson later announced the suspensions of nine students.

That was pretty much it. By March 5, the whole thing was over and I returned to Chicago to cover the city's routine mayhem—murders, fires, and battles between and among street gangs with names like Blackstone Rangers, Vice Lords, and Latin Kings.

The life of a news reporter in a city like Chicago did not, and I'm sure still doesn't meet even an elastic definition of normal; but in those years, almost no one's life in America was normal, however it might have appeared to be so on the surface. That some people today manifest a nostalgia for the sixties (which actually covered the last half of that decade and the first of the next) amazes me. It was a dreadful time. American society had come to resemble a shattered mirror still in its frame, the fissures between hawk and dove, Left and Right, old and young, black and white threatening to widen until the pieces fell out and broke into bits. The worst year was 1968: the Tet Offensive, one hundred thousand U.S. casualties in Vietnam in those twelve months; the assassinations of Martin Luther King and Bobby Kennedy;

the convention riots in Chicago, which had been rocked just months earlier by the race riots set off by King's death, with half the West Side destroyed in orgies of arson and looting, accompanied by gunfire.

I had some direct contact with both events. During the racial upheaval, I had to speed down the Eisenhower Expressway through the West Side's smoke to take my younger sister from her city apartment to our parents' house in the suburbs. Six months later, when the Democratic convention came to Chicago, I was living in a third-floor walk-up not far from Lincoln Park, marshaling grounds for the antiwar legions composed of Abbie Hoffman's Yippies and the more clean-cut but more militant Students for a Democratic Society, or SDS. There was dissension and anger inside the convention hall. Mayor Richard J. Daley, his broad, red, meaty face the face of the city that was hog butcher to the world, rose up to curse the elegant Sen. Abraham Ribicoff, who in his speech had condemned the actions of the Chicago police, which the Kerner Commission would later describe as a police riot. Outside, the situation approached anarchy—mobs of cheering, jeering, window-smashing protestors, club-wielding cops bloodying skulls while National Guardsmen lobbed tear gas grenades, the whole wild scene illuminated by the stroboscopic pulses of squad car and ambulance lights.

I had been with the *Tribune* for three months, assigned to

the suburbs to learn my craft. Coming home from my placid beat in the sticks, I parked near my apartment in a no-parking zone and propped my press card on the dashboard to avoid getting a ticket—though the police were far too busy cracking heads to bother with such trivialities. This press card was about a foot long and several inches high with white letters on a blue background that read: "Cook County Sheriff" at the top and below that, "Press."

The apartment was not air-conditioned, and I had left the windows open—Chicago in August can feel like Saigon—so the whole place stunk of tear gas. As I was closing one of the front windows, a band of militants, wearing motorcycle helmets and armed with baseball bats, came running down Sedgewick Street. The words "Cook County Sheriff" on the press card behind my car's windshield must have caught their eye. One yelled, "Pig car! Pig car!" and smashed both headlights with his club. Before I had a chance to react, he and his friends fled, pursued by a squad of Chicago's finest, whose motto was "We Serve and Protect." Because the media, in editorials and commentaries, had sharply criticized them, the cops hated reporters almost as much as they hated the demonstrators. Running past my Triumph Spitfire, one of the servant-protectors also noticed the card, but I assume the word that caught his eye was "Press." He spun around, cracked my windshield with his nightstick, then resumed pursuit of the protestors.

A police riot, sure enough.

I mention this minor incident to give some idea of what those times were like. Cops had become vandals, the forces of disorder and those of order had fused, things were spinning out of control. And the engine driving the centrifuge was the war. You could not escape it. It was on the TV news every night, on the radio, in the headlines, on people's lips and in their minds. Foremost, it was on the minds of every male under the age of twenty-six. With an unlucky number drawn in the random lottery of the draft, you could be sent to the other side of the world to kill or be killed (or maimed or driven insane) in a war that only the deluded believed to be anything but senseless and unwinnable. Richard Nixon, that glowering man with the soul of Lear, a man fully capable of causing or suffering a tragedy—and he did both—had won the 1968 presidential race. He proclaimed himself the leader of and spokesman for what he called the Silent Majority, and had pledged to extricate the United States from the Asian quagmire.

Almost two years later, we were still in Vietnam. True, American troops were being withdrawn, "Vietnamization," i.e., turning the war over to the South Vietnamese, was in progress, but the bombs continued to fall, the body bags were still coming home, if in diminishing numbers, and the draft continued to pluck young men out of small towns, neighborhoods, and farms. The American people were fed up with the war, but most—that Silent Majority—were willing to give Nixon the benefit of the doubt and a chance to work things out. Meanwhile, America's noisy minority had gotten noisier and nastier. At their fringes—or was it their leading edges?—the civil rights and antiwar movements had embraced a cult of violence. On the civil rights front, the hymn-singing Freedom Riders of the early sixties had given way to the Black Panthers and other militant groups who weren't the hymn-singing type. On the antiwar front, there had been an evolution from the candlelit peace marches of earlier years to the sort of riot that had afflicted Chicago in 1968 to, finally, protest by bomb and arson.

The New Left, as it was called, was led by the SDS, and the SDS had been hijacked by its most extreme elements. They emerged at the SDS national conference in the summer of 1969. Formed in 1960 at the University of Michigan as the student arm of an old-Left organization, the League for Industrial Democracy, the SDS had been involved in civil rights causes and in inner city community organizing projects during the early sixties. Tom Hayden, a leader of the Democratic convention protests, later a California state assemblyman and one of Jane Fonda's husbands, had been among the SDS's founders. It might have remained a small, obscure band of quasi-socialist idealists had it not been for the galvanizing effect of the Vietnam War. By 1969 it had grown to one hundred thousand members in three hundred chapters across the country.

At its national conference—another Chicago event—a factional fight erupted among the SDS mainstream, a Marxist group called Progressive Labor, and the Revolutionary Youth Movement, putative revolutionaries from middle and upper-middle class backgrounds and with long histories of student activism. In love with romantic rebels like Che Guevara, these white, disaffected undergraduates issued a manifesto called "You don't need a weatherman to tell you which way the wind blows," a title borrowed from a line in Bob Dylan's countercultural anthem, *The Subterranean Homesick Blues.*

The manifesto expressed disdain for the SDS's policies of peaceful protest (though we have seen that their demonstrations were not always peaceful); rejected Progressive Labor's call for an alliance with the white working class, which the authors considered too conservative and pro-war; and called for a campaign of "exemplary violence" by planting bombs in symbolic targets like the Pentagon, ROTC buildings, military bases, and other "imperialist" bastions.

The idea—or perhaps notion is the better word—behind these tactics was to "bring the war home," in the words of a prominent RYM leader, Mark Rudd, and to provoke a violent overthrow of the U.S. government, which in the RYM's view was the only way to change the system. Utterly divorced from political reality, they believed America was ripe for such a revolt.

Reading an account of the conference in the Chicago papers, I recall thinking that as a political theory, "exemplary violence" was the sort of rubbish one would expect from privileged white youth who had no experience of real violence and its effects—ragged bullet wounds, headless torsos, dismembered and eviscerated corpses, pain and grief.

The group changed its name to "Weathermen," and, led by charismatic and photogenic figures like Bernardine Dohrn, William Ayers, Kathy Boudin, David Gilbert, and Bill Flanagan, staged its first example of exemplary violence in Chicago in October 1969. It was called the "Days of Rage."

The Weathermen's intent was to transform themselves from bourgeois kids into revolutionary street fighters by taking on the Chicago police in hand-to-hand combat, and through their actions rally others to their flag. In the event, they would prove to be no match for Irish, Italian, and Polish cops who had learned street fighting in first grade. Things got off to a rousing start on October 6, when Ayers (prep school graduate, son of a utility company executive, raised in the affluent suburb of Glen Ellyn) and a few others blew up a statue in Haymarket Square dedicated to police killed and injured in the 1886 Haymarket Riot.

The "official" Days of Rage protest began two days later.

I was on the rewrite desk and took dictation from *Tribune* reporters on the street. The Weathermen had expected thousands to show up, but mustered a mere five hundred. They were armed with brass knuckles, clubs, lead pipes, and chains, and were garbed in goggles, gas masks, and football helmets (thus turning an iconic image of the all-American jock on its head). The inversion was carried further in the stadium cheers they yelled as they ran down the streets: "Ho, Ho, Ho Chi Minh! NLF is gonna win!" and "What do you want? Revolution! When do you want it? Now!" A bank window was shattered, and that started a bacchanalia of glass breaking. The cops waded in, and in less than an hour had shot and slightly wounded six Weathermen, arrested seventy more, and clubbed an unknown number.

The next day, those Weathermen not in jail or too seriously hurt to continue tried again. This time the battle lasted only half an hour. Some two hundred were taken in, bloodied and bruised. The only casualty on the establishment side was an overeager city official who was paralyzed from the neck down when he dove to tackle a protester and crashed headfirst into a brick wall.

Thus ended "The Days of Rage." It was almost comic. Mike Royko, the great columnist for the *Chicago Daily News*, told me over a beer in the Billy Goat tavern that the Weathermen weren't capable "of fighting their way out of a Polish wedding." He used the line in his column the next day.

It seemed the Weathermen agreed with Royko's assessment. The drubbing they'd suffered gave them second thoughts about engaging in direct combat. They decided that their strategy would be more effective if carried out underground, and began to build a clandestine network that would blow things up and burn things down. They became terrorists, providing an example of how passionate convictions can mutate into a nihilistic murderousness.

Bernardine Dohrn issued a "Declaration of war on the United States government" in December, when the Weathermen returned to Chicago to take part in demonstrations protesting the death of Fred Hampton, a young, spellbinding leader of the Black Panthers. The Weathermen had been seeking an alliance with the Panthers, which spurned them as dangerous dilettantes. Hampton had said "these kids are going to get people massacred," a bitterly ironic comment because it was Hampton who got massacred in a gun battle with Cook County State's Attorney's officers. Actually, it was questionable if a gun battle had taken place. State's Attorney Edward Hanrahan declared that his men had been fired on when they raided Hampton's West Side apartment to arrest him and search for illegal weapons, but there were indications that the two groups of police, one at the front door, one at back, had been shooting at each other. An indiscriminate fusillade from semiautomatic weapons and revolvers ripped through the apartment, killing Hampton in bed.

I had covered the aftermath of the shooting, and wondered if Chicago had become the epicenter of the quake that was cracking the social and cultural soil all across America.

In March 1970, the Weathermen—now rechristened the Weather Underground—resurfaced in spectacular, if self-destructive, fashion. One of their cells, which was called "focos," had hatched a plot to plant a nail bomb at a dance in the Officer's Mess at Fort Dix, New Jersey. Had this act of exemplary violence occurred, it would have killed and injured not only army officers but their wives and dates as well. Fortunately for the intended victims, the Underground was as inept at bomb-making as it was at street fighting. The device blew up in the Manhattan town house in which it was being constructed, killing Ayers's girlfriend, Diana Oughten, and two other Weathermen. Ayers, Rudd, Dohrn, et al., ended up on the FBI's Ten Most Wanted Fugitives list and went on the lam.

So far they had succeeded only in killing themselves and in alienating the rest of the SDS. As one SDS member at the University of Wisconsin remarked, "You don't need a rectal thermometer to know where the assholes are." Nevertheless, their aura of outlaw glamour had drawn some flattering profiles in the press, while their violent rhetoric and actions had won them a number of admirers and copycats in the antiwar movement, among whom an idea, a feeling, took hold that no antiwar demonstration could be authentic if it wasn't violent, that civil disobedience should be as uncivil as possible. The Apollonian had surrendered to the Dionysian.

The old karma was at work. Violence begets violence begets more violence. The unprovoked gunfire poured into Hampton's apartment was a preview of things to come. Federal law enforcement agencies were also of a mind to take extraordinary measures. In its pursuit of the Weather Underground fugitives, the FBI broke so many laws that, when they were finally brought to trial, the cases against most of them were thrown out of court.

The atmosphere in the country had grown toxic with hate. The Black Panthers hated whites, the white Weathermen hated American society, the cops hated them all, and each Friday night Walter Cronkite announced the weekly toll in Vietnam, which everyone hated. The tension was more than palpable—you could practically smell it, hear it in the pop music of the day—the angry, jarring riffs of Jimi Hendrix's amped-up guitar, in the death-haunted lyrics of songs like *Fortunate Son* and *Bad Moon Risin'*.

Don't go out tonight, it's bound to take your life
There's a bad moon on the rise.

And there was—a bad moon, a bad mood, one of ominous expectancy. There seemed to be a yearning in the national psyche—if there is such a thing—for a catharsis. America was ready for a tragedy, and on May 4, 1970, it got one.

Whoever directed this production picked an odd venue—the campus of a little-known, midsize state college in northeastern Ohio. The curtain was raised five days earlier and far away in Indochina, where twenty thousand American and South Vietnamese troops, under President Nixon's direct orders, invaded Cambodia to destroy major North Vietnamese and Vietcong bases across the border. Nixon announced the invasion—it was called an "incursion"—in a televised address on the night of April 30. As described by Stanley Karnow in *Vietnam: A History*, the president's mood at the time was consonant with the mood in the country: tense, paranoid, ugly. Public reaction to his decision varied. Most of the Silent Majority, exhibiting their traditional loyalty to the chief executive, registered support by remaining silent. Opinion makers, however, raised their voices. As Karnow notes, "Educators, clergymen, lawyers, businessmen, and others protested." Karnow might have added that so did a number of more ordinary citizens, organizing peace marches in comfortable bedroom communities like Scarsdale, New York. There was dissent even in the administration. Walter Hickel, Nixon's secretary of the interior, openly objected to the invasion, for which he was fired. Two hundred members of the State Department expressed their disagreement in a public petition. *The New York Times* editorialized that the action was a "virtual renunciation" of Nixon's promise to end the war. The conservative *Wall Street Journal* warned against a deeper entrapment in Southeast Asia.

The unrest simmering on university campuses burst into angry demonstrations all over the country the next day, a Friday. I wasn't paying close attention to the one at Kent State, if I was paying any at all. At the time, my first wife, Jill, and I were living in the old, shady suburb of Oak Park, our rented flat a couple of blocks from some fine examples of Frank Lloyd Wright architecture and Hemingway's birthplace. I have no memory of what I did that weekend. I'd probably spent the mornings working on the manuscript that would become *A Rumor of War* and the afternoons either watching football games or fixing up a spare room as a nursery for our first child, expected that August.

Before reporting in to the newsroom Monday morning, I got a call from the day city editor. The disturbances in Kent, Ohio, had grown serious over the weekend. Store windows had been smashed in town, radicals had burned down the ROTC building, firemen had been driven off by mobs slashing hoses and throwing stones, and the Kent city police were unable to cope with the situation. The Ohio National Guard had been ordered in and were now occupying the university. The national desk wanted me to get there immediately. Evidently my coverage of the University of Illinois demonstrations the month before qualified me as the paper's campus protest correspondent.

My first question was, "Where the hell is Kent State?" I had never heard of it. Informed of its location, I booked the next available flight to Cleveland, packed a bag, said goodbye to Jill, and drove to O'Hare Airport. During the hourlong flight, I read a wire-service story to bring myself up to date. Ohio's governor, James A. Rhodes, had blamed the disturbances on "outside agitators." I had learned to be skeptical about such claims, but was willing to set my skepticism aside. The burning of the ROTC building was right out of the Weather Underground's handbook. Except for that—and it was no small exception—the protests appeared to be like those at Illinois. Maybe there was one other difference. Illinois Governor Ogilvie had taken pains to calm the situation at Champaign-Urbana. Governor Rhodes adopted the opposite, a combative approach. At a press conference on Sunday he'd compared the protestors to Nazi brown shirts, describing them as "the worst sort of people we harbor in America," and promised to "use every weapon possible to eradicate the problem." A bit of political grandstanding perhaps—Rhodes was then involved in a tough primary fight for the Republican party's senatorial nomination—but it struck me as an inflammatory statement.

My memory is patchy. I believe the shootings took place while I was flying to Cleveland and that the report I heard on my rented car's radio was an update. My immediate reaction was the one you would expect: I was stunned. The next was also one you would expect from a newsman, though it now makes me cringe to recall it: *This is one helluva story and I'd better get on it.* Doing at least twenty over the limit, I arrived in Kent.

When a horror occurs in a commonplace setting, the horror is magnified. Kent could have been any college town in any part of the Midwest: the usual girdle of motels and restaurants on the outskirts, the usual elm-shaded streets lined with clapboard and shingle-sided houses, the usual student beer halls with the usual names downtown. It was at the gate to the university that the unusual appeared: an armored personnel carrier, the unit's designation stamped in white on its olive green steel, 107CAV. Rhodes had sent in the cavalry, as if the demonstrators were hostile Sioux. Further on, I encountered a barricade manned by Ohio state troopers, their patrol car windshields taped to prevent shattering in case they were hit by rocks. A trooper asked for identification, I showed my *Tribune* press card, and was waved through.

Driving on, the atmosphere of unreality thickened. The campus was deserted, the university having been closed, students and faculty sent home. In their place were National Guardsmen in full battle dress, rifles loaded, bayonets fixed.

Some troops were lined up for chow at the mess area, near the gutted ruins of the ROTC building. Others marched in formation down the sidewalks. Closer to the scene of the shooting—Taylor Hall and the practice field below it— soldiers had taken up combat positions, squatting behind trees or lying prone, scanning the field and the parking lot as if looking for snipers. The overall impression was of an occupied town in some as yet unnamed war.

No problem finding a parking space. I walked to the practice field, where I'd spotted a civilian, the only one around. He was young, in a jacket and tie. Not a student, in other words. I went up to him, thinking he might be a faculty member. He turned out to be another reporter, John Kifner from *The New York Times*. A newspaper superpower then as it is today, *The Times* did not regard a regional power like the *Tribune* as competition. Still, I thought Kifner was quite generous to give me a thorough fill-in on what had happened. That will be described in more detail later in this narrative. For now, I'll confine myself to a summary of what Kifner told me.

Several hundred demonstrators had gathered on the Commons at noon on May 4 for a scheduled antiwar rally. Several hundred more were cheering them on or merely watching them and a troop of National Guardsmen posted nearby. The guardsmen were ordered to disperse the crowd and did so, firing tear gas canisters.

After clearing the Commons, the guardsmen marched to the practice field. Protestors were gathered in the Prentice Hall parking lot, others stood in front of Taylor. More tear gas was fired, to which students responded by throwing stones and shouting obscenities at the guardsmen.

The action was over in five or ten minutes. Protestors and spectators began to straggle off. An officer ordered the soldiers to return to the Commons area. As they did, some students continued to hurl rocks and four-letter words. Suddenly, a line of guardsmen wheeled, and making no distinction among active demonstrators, bystanders, and students merely walking to class, knelt and fired, killing four, wounding nine.

I have given the dry facts Kifner gave me then, and the dry facts alone were shocking. The response to a provocation cannot always be proportionate, but to answer stones and bad language with a random volley of .30-caliber bullets was not imaginable in America. Or maybe it was, because America had changed.

I mentioned hearing on the radio that the guard's adjutant general had said that the troops fired after they had been shot at by a sniper. Kifner shook his head. No witnesses had heard a shot, nor had he, and he'd been with the students. Nevertheless, guard officers had seized on "evidence" that there had been a sniper on the roof of Taylor Hall. This was a bullet hole in an abstract steel sculpture at one end of the field. We went over to look at it—a bullet hole, all right, but you didn't need ballistics training to see that the round had been fired from ground level. It had come from a soldier's rifle.

Alone, I went to the parking lot, and in the clean spring light, saw still-distinct bloodstains in the asphalt. Whose? I wondered. Which young life had leaked out to soak into this dull pavement? I heard an echo from the Days of Rage. *What do you want? Revolution! When do you want it? Now!* Well, this is what revolutions look like, this is what they come to—bayonets, bullets, and blood, the blood of innocents, and do you still want it, now or at any time?

The next day, I went to interview the wounded, and I reproduce here one of their stories.

Wounded Kent Student Says Troops Erred

By Philip Caputo
[Chicago Tribune Press Service]

Kent, Ohio, May 5—Douglas Wrentmore is a 20-year-old sophomore who has studied psychology at Kent State university for the last two years.

In the space of about five seconds yesterday he learned about things he never learned during those two years of reading textbooks: violence and death and how it feels to be shot by a rifle. It was an experience he said he will carry with him all his life.

Wrentmore was wounded in the leg yesterday when Ohio National Guardsmen fired into a crowd of student demonstrators, killing four and wounding nine others, two of whom are in critical condition in Robinson Memorial, Ravenna, Ohio.

Wrentmore was struck in the knee. He is in fair condition and considers himself lucky.

Tells His Story

"I was in the parking lot near Taylor Hall just watching the demonstration," he said. "The guardsmen, about 50 to 75 of them, had just had a confrontation with the students in the practice football field, and they were marching away. All of a sudden I heard a volley of shots. Girls started screaming. I saw people fall, and I started running and then I fell. I didn't feel anything. One minute I could run and then I could not. Then I saw blood coming from my leg."

Wrentmore said that as he lay on the asphalt, he looked up and saw a line of about 10 guardsmen kneeling and firing into the mass of students, who numbered between 500 and 600.

"The volley wasn't preceded by a sniper's bullet. I heard later that there was supposed to have been one from the roof, but I never heard it. Anyhow, if it came from the roof, I just don't understand why the troops fired into the crowd," he said.

He added that prior to the shooting, the guardsmen were pelted with rocks and sticks by the demonstrators. However, those throwing the objects amounted to no more than a dozen, Wrentmore said. He described the rocks as "just pebbles, with a few maybe the size of a golf ball." Brig. Gen. Robert Canterbury, the guard commander, said baseball-sized rocks and concrete slabs were thrown at his troops.

Taken to Hospital

Wrentmore is not embittered by the experience. After some students helped him into a car, he was taken to the hospital, where he saw the other casualties brought in—the wounded moaning with pain, the dead wheeled in beneath blankets.

Wrentmore shifted in his bed saying, "my leg is starting to hurt now; it is stiffening up." Then he looked at the cast, tapping it with his finger as though to convince himself that it was really there, and that all he saw and heard the day before had really happened.

At a press conference later in the day, Brigadier General Canterbury, seemingly impervious to doubt and incapable of contrition, reiterated his statements about rocks as big as baseballs and concrete slabs being thrown at his troops. He said that some protestors were as close as three feet to the guardsmen. This was curious, as it had already been determined that some victims had been as far as seven hundred feet away. A major-league center fielder could not have thrown a rock that distance. The closest student, who was wounded, had been sixty to seventy feet from the line of fire, a long way to heave a concrete slab. Nevertheless, Canterbury, who had been with the troops, insisted that their lives had been in danger and that they had fired in self-defense. "The situation was dangerous," he said. "I felt I could be killed."

The press conference over, I went to the mess area, found a lieutenant who had commanded a platoon on the hill by Taylor Hall, and asked for his version of events. I have a vague recollection of a man of about twenty-five, with reddish hair and freckles, but my memory could be wrong. He granted an interview on condition I not use his name. I have a clipping of the story I wrote, and this is what he told me:

"We were surrounded and outnumbered ten to one. You should have seen those animals. They were trying to take our rifles away. Someone in the crowd yelled that we were only carrying blanks, so the students assaulted up the hill while others tried to outflank us by going around the rear of Taylor Hall."

Viewing their situation as desperate, he went on, seventeen guardsmen turned, some dropping to one knee, the rest standing, and without orders loosed a thirty-five-shot volley. It would be determined later that the actual figures were twenty-eight soldiers and sixty-seven shots, but the lieutenant's statistical inaccuracies could be overlooked. What struck me was his choice of language: "surrounded and outnumbered ten to one," "assaulted up the hill," "tried to outflank us." It almost sounded like a scene from the movie *Zulu*—the thin red line attacked by hordes of spear-carrying savages.

I recall thinking, "This is complete crap." No one else I'd spoken to had seen students attempting to disarm the guardsmen—they weren't close enough even if they'd wanted to. No one had heard a yell that the soldiers had blank rounds in their rifles. And the picture of college kids conducting a complex military maneuver, some making a frontal assault while others conducted a flanking movement, was pure fantasy.

From my experience in Vietnam I knew something about real combat and what it was like to fear for your life, and felt angry. If the guardsmen had perceived themselves to be in danger, then something was seriously wrong with their perceptions or, more likely, with their training, discipline, and leadership. The lieutenant was lying to me because he was lying to himself, creating a story he could live with, or maybe to protect himself and others from legal action.

As a journalist, I had to keep my opinions to myself, but to my mind, the guardsmen had panicked and committed manslaughter or reckless homicide. Before they were dispatched to Kent State, they'd quelled a Teamsters Union strike in Akron. Teamsters are more formidable adversaries than undergraduates, and the strike had been marked by deadly violence, including gunplay between striking truckers and strike breakers. Thrust from that to a campus in turmoil, seeing the ROTC building burned to the ground, the part-time soldiers had been tired and on edge. Nor can one ignore the effect Governor Rhodes's vow to "use every weapon to eradicate the problem" must have had on them. I thought the Kent State faculty had it right in a resolution passed on May 5 condemning the shootings: "We hold the guardsmen, acting under orders and under psychological pressures less responsible than are Gov. Rhodes and Adjutant General (Sylvester) Del Corso, whose inflammatory indoctrination produced these pressures."

Kent townspeople generally supported the guard's actions. As in most college communities, there was a "town-gown" conflict between Kent's 27,000 citizens and the university's 21,000 students, but it was warped into outright hostility by the events of the previous week and by the temper of the times. Many Kent citizens hated the students, regarding them as an alien race. You could hardly blame them for their anger—stores and businesses downtown had been vandalized for no reason. That said, some townsfolk went far over the top with comments like, "They should have shot more of them."

On May 6, the inspector general of the Ohio National Guard announced that his office was investigating the shootings. So was the U.S. Department of Justice, while on the local level the Porter County coroner had opened an inquiry into the four deaths. These would be the first of many probes into what soon became known as the Kent State Massacre. Like the Boston Massacre almost exactly two hundred years before (March 5, 1770), which it resembled, it was called a massacre not for the number of its victims but for the wanton manner in which they were shot down. Its anthem became the Crosby, Stills, Nash, and Young song *Ohio*, its iconic emblem the photograph snapped by John Filo, a Kent State student and freelance photographer, in the Prentice Hall parking lot. It shows Mary Vecchio, a fourteen-year-old runaway, screaming with upraised hands as she kneels over the body of Jeffrey Miller.

The 107th Cavalry withdrew from Kent State and so did I, summoned back to Chicago to cover yet another protest at Northwestern University in suburban Evanston. Border to border, sea to shining sea, hundreds of student strikes and demonstrations had sprung up in reaction to the shootings.

When I got to Northwestern, barely having had time to say hello to my pregnant wife, I found red flags of revolt hanging from the windows of dormitories, frat houses, and classroom buildings. At strike headquarters, on the third floor of Scott Hall, coeds were painting signs calling for an end to the war—as their mothers or older sisters in years past might have painted signs urging the NU Wildcats to beat Wisconsin. Sound trucks blared rock music. In front of the Technological Institute, physics professors sold black arm-bands to symbolize mourning for the dead in Ohio. One, Dr. Martin Block, hawked them with a sense of humor: "Arm-bands. Armbands. Any contribution will do. Help a physics professor." The lighthearted pitch belied his emotions. "The protest movement in the academic community got going again with the Cambodia involvement," he told me. "The Kent State incident was like a bomb going off, and the echoes of that explosion are being heard across the country."

Across the street, the less politicized had taken advantage of the strike to play tennis. Looking at the tanned players in their crisp whites, listening to the *thwack-thwack* of the ball, I felt that I was squinting through a telescope turned back-ward to the past. It was a picture of what college campuses had been like only a few years before, but that tranquil time now seemed as distant as the days of raccoon coats and rum-ble seats.

A brief walk through the handsome campus brought me

back to the troubled present. The scene could have been lifted from a Delacroix painting of the French Revolution. A young man stood atop a barricade of furniture and cars and sawhorses, his long hair tousled by the Lake Michigan wind, one hand grasping a pole flying a red flag and an upside-down American flag (a distress signal) as he exhorted some twenty-five hundred students massed behind him to "Strike! Strike!"

Suddenly, he was interrupted by a burly, black-haired, middle-age man dressed in a workingman's khaki trousers and a flannel shirt. Mounting the barricade, he tried to wrest the flagpole from the student. "That's my flag!" he yelled. "I fought for it. You have no right to it."

The young man jerked it away and leaped into the crowd. The older man jumped after him and a tug-of-war took place, accompanied by shouts and epithets. Some dissenters threatened to break his jaw, others urged, "No, no. Don't sink to that level."

After some struggle, a few students managed to take the angry man aside to engage him in a dialogue. He said something about fighting on Iwo Jima and that he was an electrician. One undergraduate said, "We can talk to you, man. We can talk to each other." It soon became apparent that they could not. The students argued that the man, as a member of the working class, was a victim of capitalism. Students and blacks were also victims of capitalism. Therefore, he should join their movement.

The Marxist language sounded incongruous, if not absurd in that setting—Northwestern was the most affluent school in the Big Ten, Evanston an aviary for capitalists—and this member of the working class was having none of it.

"The hell with your movement," he said. "There are millions of people like me. We're fed up with your movement. You're forcing us into it. We'll have to kill you."

"Like they did at Kent!" screamed several students, almost in unison. "Like they did at Kent! You want to kill us all."

"Kent is the logical outcome of what you've been doing for the last five years," he shot back. "What else did you expect?"

I stood taking notes. If I hadn't known better, I would have thought this bit of street theater, so illustrative of the passions dividing America, had been staged for my benefit.

The electrician put his hands on his hips, shook his head, and started to walk away. Then he turned abruptly, pointing his finger at the crowd pressing around him. "It's time for action," he declared. "I'm through arguing. I came here to resist your movement."

One student opened his mouth to say something, but another motioned for him to be silent and cried out, "Oh, fuck him. You can't talk to him."

"And I can't talk to you. All I can see is a lot of kids blowing the chance I never had."

Then the representative of Nixon's Silent Majority, having broken his silence, spun around and walked off, his back

to the wildly dressed protestors and the scarlet banners flut-
tering from the barricade separating two worlds that spoke
the same language but could not understand each other.

There is a postscript to my experiences with the Kent
State massacre and its aftermath. Sometime later in May, I
covered a meeting of Kent State alumni at the Sheraton-
O'Hare hotel on the far northwest side of Chicago. It was a
strained gathering. The alumni, old, young, and in between,
sipped martinis and talked about football games won and
lost, about former professors and campus pranks, and it was
obvious they were trying extremely hard to pretend that this
was just another get-together of former classmates. It didn't
work. There was something artificial in their voices, some
note of insincerity in their laughter, like the tinkling of glass
that is being passed off as crystal. They knew what they
were going to hear from the featured speaker, and it wasn't
going to deal with honors day or graduation day or how
much new construction was taking place at their alma
mater.

At the appointed time, they sat down to listen as Dr.
Donald Roskens, vice president of administration, rose to
the lectern.

"That violence begets violence was no more dramatically
illustrated than during those first three days at Kent State, a
prologue to the armed tragedy that took place on the
fourth," he said. "And on that day, the victory bell tolled

sadly as a postlude to death." He went on, telling the alumni how those at Kent State had lived for the entire world an experience of what it means to find academic freedom extinguished, to live in a military state, to know what results from "terror, threats, and violence." It was plain that he meant that not all the terror and violence had come from the Ohio National Guard. He wound up with a call to alumni, students, and faculty to rebuild a sense of community at the university, and with a plea for moderation: "We must draw from the cacophony of both extremes the chords of harmony."

It would be a long time before anyone heard those sweet, harmonious chords.

Chapter 2

Chapter 2

From a story I filed from Kent State:

University officials tonight disclosed the academic records of the four slain students. Allison Krause, 19, of Pittsburgh, was an art history major with a B average. Jeffrey Glenn Miller, 20, of Plainview, N.Y., was a psychology major with a C average. Sandra Lee Scheuer, 20, of Youngstown, O., was majoring in speech and hearing with a B average. William K. Schroeder, a psychology major from Lorain, O., was a dean's list student with a 3.2 grade point average.

To the public at large, they were names, with perhaps a photograph and a thumbnail biography in the newspapers or *Time* or *Newsweek*. Today, outside of Kent State, you will have a hard time finding anyone who remembers who they were, except for their classmates and their families, their families most of all, for whom the platitudes of modern pop-therapy—"closure," "the healing process"—must sound like obscenities. To lose a child is horrible; to lose a child in the way they lost theirs must bring an anguish and a rage none of us can imagine, a spiritual wound no one can close or heal.

Krause, Miller, Scheuer, and Schroeder—victims of what Dr. Roskens called "the armed tragedy."

Overuse and misuse have stripped the word "tragedy" of meaning. Plane crashes, deadly highway collisions, earthquakes, floods, and fires resulting in fatalities are called tragedies all the time, but they're not. They're accidents or natural disasters. In its dictionary definition, a tragedy is a literary form. "A play or other literary work of a serious or sorrowful character, with a fatal or disastrous conclusion," according to the *Oxford Universal Dictionary*. *Webster's* is more expansive: "A serious play or drama typically dealing with the problems of a central character, leading to an unhappy or disastrous ending brought on, as in ancient drama, by fate and a tragic flaw in this character, or, in modern drama, usually by moral weakness, psychological maladjustment, or social pressures."

I have worked out my own definition of tragedies that occur offstage, in real life: "An event caused by a combination of blind circumstance and human folly, weakness or ignorance that ends in death." If that definition is accurate, then all real-life tragedies are works of collaboration; they have many authors, but some of those authors are more responsible for the final work than others.

It is necessary to put flesh and bones and personalities on those names struck into a marble slab on a hill in Ohio. Lives, not identities, were extinguished on that May afternoon. Extending Dr. Rosken's symphonic metaphor, we'll begin with the prelude.

It is noon, May 1. In a symbolic protest of the Cambodian invasion announced one day prior, about five hundred students congregate on the Commons, a broad, grassy area in the heart of the Kent State campus, where various kinds of assemblies have traditionally been held, from pep rallies to political demonstrations. Impassioned speeches opposing the war and the Nixon administration are made, and then a graduate student buries a copy of the U.S. Constitution to signify its death because Congress never declared war on Indochina. Before the rally breaks up, protest leaders announce that another is scheduled for noon on Monday, the fourth.

Two hours later, the Black United Students hold a rally, but it's not related to the war. Problems in the black community and racial incidents at Ohio State University are discussed. It, too, is peaceful. Aware that emotions are running high, the university's president, Robert White, has been keeping a careful eye on the situation; faculty marshals have been appointed to make sure demonstrations don't get out of hand. The campus is calm, however, with most students getting ready for dates, leaving for the weekend (William

Schroeder is one), or planning for a night in town, where they'll watch the NBA basketball playoffs in local bars. White decides to leave on a planned trip to Iowa.

At around 11:00 p.m., the balmy spring night and alcohol conspire with antiwar sentiments to create disorder. A crowd of young people, some of whom are not Kent State students, swarms onto Water Street and close it to traffic. At first, this looks like youthful high spirits getting a bit out of hand. A local motorcycle gang joins in, doing wheelies and other tricks on their bikes. A bonfire is set, then one group begins to trash stores and deface property. Caught off guard, the Kent city police do nothing to stop the disturbances. Soon, windows are being broken. Called at his home, Mayor Leroy Satrom is told what's going on. He declares "a state of emergency" and orders the bars closed and the police to clear the streets.

The law of unintended consequences takes effect. Instead of calming the situation, the mayor's directive aggravates it. Bar patrons, many unaware of what's been happening outside, pour into the streets, resentful that their evening has been disrupted. The cops don't distinguish between participants and bystanders, harassing or arresting the latter, and the mood of hostility grows. By this time—between 12:30 and 1:00 a.m.—the vandalism has taken on a definite political coloration: "establishment" businesses, like the bank and the gas company have been targeted.

Around one in the morning, the Kent police attempt to drive the crowd out of downtown and toward the campus, but the Kent State campus police offer virtually no assistance in this effort, for reasons that have not been determined. Finally, about half an hour later, the crowd breaks up, having caused some $15,000 in damages to town shops and businesses.

Saturday is the day for rumors and vague but troubling reports. The Kent chief of police, Edward Thompson, tells Mayor Satrom that his undercover officers have observed strange faces in town. Merchants report receiving anonymous threats that their businesses will be damaged if they don't place antiwar messages in their windows. There is even a rumor that the city water supply is going to be spiked with LSD and that carloads of SDS militants are soon to arrive in Kent. The mayor, afraid that his police force will be facing unrest beyond its capacities, first imposes a confusing curfew—8:00 p.m. to 6:00 a.m. in town, 11:00 p.m. to 6:00 a.m. on campus—and later requests Governor Rhodes to send in the National Guard, which had been placed on alert the previous night. For reasons that are not clear to this day, he fails to inform university officials of this decision.

Like Satrom and Thompson, university officials find themselves in a situation they had not anticipated or prepared for. Kent State has a core of dedicated activist students and an SDS chapter, but it is by no stretch of the imagination a "radical" campus. Its student body are children of ordinary people, small businessmen and skilled blue-collar workers like Jeffrey Miller's father, Bernie, a linotype operator. At the height of its popularity, the Kent State SDS never had more than two to three hundred members—1 percent of total enrollment—and it held little appeal. Indeed, when the SDS attempted to disrupt a meeting of the Kent State board of trustees in 1969 to present demands to abolish ROTC, they were blocked not only by KSU police but by about seven hundred anti-SDS students. As journalist I. F. Stone was to remark in *The New York Review of Books* several months after the shootings, "This is a campus where you meet activists who have never heard of *The Nation* or read *The New Republic* and students who think themselves avant-garde because they read *Time* and *Newsweek*."

Nevertheless, radicalism comes to it on Saturday night, May 2, when between six hundred and one thousand people gather on the Commons. A few Kent high school students are mixed in with the college students, and again, strangers are observed at the gathering. After a while, most leave the area, but one band attempts to set fire to the nearby ROTC building, tossing matches into the old, wooden structure. After several tries, they succeed, and by 9:00 p.m., the building is ablaze. Like all fires, it draws a lot of spectators, who become so intermingled with the demonstrators that no one can tell the one from the other. The Kent fire department arrives, but is soon driven off as rioting protestors slash hoses and stone the firemen. The campus police don't even attempt to protect them or to disperse the crowd, which begins to sweep toward the Prentice Gate as the building burns to the ground.

The National Guard, whose arrival surprises students and faculty alike, blocks the gate, which leads from campus into town, and with fixed bayonets gains control of the situation. A little before midnight, Brigadier General Canterbury can report that the disturbances are over, at least for now.

It still isn't known who set the fire to the ROTC building. There are a couple of theories, but whoever did it can claim a share of responsibility for what happened two days later. It escalated the level of violence and heightened tensions. One can imagine the reaction of the guardsmen, pulled off the trucker's strike to quell what they thought was a student demonstration, and then coming upon a scene that must have looked like a full-blown civil insurrection: the night sky an inferno, hordes of angry students attempting to storm the gate to the city.

But the guard became the arsonists' collaborators. The university authorities having done nothing to apprehend those who started the fire or to protect the firemen, the guardsmen proceeded to do too much, ranging through campus firing tear gas, sweeping up everyone in their path, regardless of what they were doing. A couple of students suffered minor bayonet wounds.

On Sunday morning, with six hundred soldiers on campus and four hundred more in town, Kent and the university look like what they are—communities under military occupation. Now it is time for Governor Rhodes to add his byline to the list of authors who will write the May 4 tragedy. He arrives in Kent at 10:00 a.m. and holds a press conference at which he makes his famous remark that the events of the past two days have been caused by outside agitators who are "worse than brown shirts, worse than communists, the worst type of people we harbor in America," and then vows to use every weapon possible to "eradicate the problem." Since these unidentified people *are* the problem, it is easy to see why his words strike some as meaning, "we are going to eradicate *them*." He sounds like Joseph Conrad's Mister Kurtz in *Heart of Darkness*, scrawling in his diary his solution to the problem of rebellious natives in the Congo— *Exterminate the brutes.*

Before returning to the capital in Columbus, Rhodes indicates that he is going to declare a state of emergency, which leads university officials and guard officers alike to conclude—incorrectly, it turns out—that martial law has been imposed and that any further rallies or gatherings are prohibited.

While all this is going on, Allison Krause is strolling the

campus with her friend Barry Levine. Both are activists, but closer to the peaceful, "flower child" type than they are to the Weathermen. The focus of their antiwar sentiments has shifted from far-off Cambodia to Kent State; they want the National Guard to leave. This is something they share with most of their classmates; regardless of where they stand on the war, KSU students feel that they have been invaded.

A guardsman standing alone catches Krause's eye—there is a lilac in his rifle barrel. Taking Levine by the hand, she walks over to the soldier and engages him in conversation. This is not an unusual thing for her to do. She has a gift for establishing rapport with strangers. Once, while working a summer job at a hospital for the insane, she coaxed a patient to talk who hadn't spoken a word in fifteen years. Slender, with long, wavy dark hair, Krause is winsome and quick-witted, and her charm has an immediate effect on the guardsman. He smiles and says that his name is Meyers and that he doesn't want to be on the campus any more than the students want him there. Krause, naive about military discipline, then asks why he doesn't leave. He tells her why.

At this point, as Levine will later relate in a letter to Krause's parents, an officer approaches and places an arm around Meyers's shoulder. The young soldier's smile fades, his face tightens, his back straightens. In a loud voice, the officer asks if Meyers's division has target practice next week. Meyers replies that it does. The following exchange then takes place.

"Are you going there with that silly flower?"

"No, sir."

"Then what is it doing in your rifle barrel?"

"It was a gift, sir."

"Do you always accept gifts, Meyers?"

"No, sir."

"Then why did you accept this one?"

Meyers doesn't answer. The officer holds out his hand.

"What are you going to do with it, Meyers?"

The soldier removes the lilac and gives it to the officer.

"That's better, Meyers. Now straighten out and start acting like a soldier and forget all this peace stuff."

On an impulse, Krause snatches the flower from the officer's hand. This isn't like her—she tends to avoid direct confrontation, and can be stoic to the point of passivity in the face of provocative words or actions. The officer turns his back and walks away, and Krause calls after him, "What's the matter with peace? Flowers are better than bullets."

Krause's chat with Guardsman Meyers is not unique. All across the campus on this warm, breezy Sunday, students are conversing with soldiers. The atmosphere contrasts sharply with Governor Rhodes's bellicose remarks at the press conference, but then, he's trailing his primary rival by eight points and needs the law-and-order vote.

Despite the cordial chats, friction grows. At 8:00 that night, a few hundred students gather on the Commons to protest Kent State's "occupation."

Guard officers announce the imposition of a new curfew replacing Mayor Satrom's. The students refuse to move. They are later dispersed with tear gas. Soldiers move through campus, and once again students who are merely walking between dorms or to and from the library are swept up, deepening and broadening resentment. Epithets are hurled at the guardsmen, who are growing exasperated with being cursed, stoned, and confronted by students who refuse to obey.

Attempting to demonstrate that the curfew is unnecessary, protestors march to the Prentice Gate, where, as on Saturday night, they are met by guardsmen. They then stage a sit-in and ask that both the mayor and the university president speak to them about the guard's presence on campus. They are told their request will be granted, but two hours later are informed that neither official will meet with them, that the curfew is in effect, and that they must disperse immediately. They refuse. Now helicopters are called in and fly overhead with searchlights blazing, the throb of their rotors sounding like an echo from the war raging ten thousand miles away. Again with tear gas and bayonets, the guard breaks up the crowd. Fifty-one people are arrested.

William Schroeder has returned to Kent State from his

weekend away. He has not joined in the protests, although this ROTC student has begun to question the war in general and the Cambodian invasion in particular. The atmosphere on campus is ugly and ominous, and as helicopters beat through the night sky, their searchlights piercing his dorm window, he leans out of his bunk before going to sleep and tells his roommate, Lou Cusella, "I'm scared, Louie." Those will be the last words Cusella ever hears Schroeder speak.

From midnight to mid Monday morning, all is quiet. At 10:00 a.m., a meeting of local, state, and university authorities is convened in Kent. Some of those present, still under the mistaken impression that Governor Rhodes has declared martial law, argue that the rally scheduled for noon is illegal. Others disagree, but for reasons that will never be made clear, no one bothers to call the governor's office for a clarification. It is simply assumed martial law was his intent. A consensus is reached to ban the rally to avoid heightening tensions and prevent further violence. Kent State officials print twelve thousand leaflets announcing the prohibition, but distribution is so poorly handled that most students never see the leaflets. Indeed, it appears that some faculty marshals are in the dark.

At 11:00 a.m. about two hundred demonstrators assemble near the victory bell at one end of the Commons. It hangs in a small brick structure vaguely resembling a pagoda

and is usually rung to signal a football victory. Today it is
rung to summon students to the rally. As on the previous
night's sit-in, the war has taken a backseat to the issue of the
National Guard's occupation of the campus. Now circumstances, or fate, add a few lines to the drama's script. The
class break occurs at 11:45 a.m. Because of the central location and the approaching noon hour, the Commons fills
with students, some on their way to class, some heading to
dorms or the student union for lunch, some pausing to
watch the protest or to cheer the demonstrators on. As many
as three thousand people swarm through the area. The
guard unit at the end of the Commons opposite the victory
bell is a single troop, ninety-six men, and although they have
live ammunition in their M-1 clips and ample supplies of
tear gas, they are nervous. There is a disparity between the
facts and the soldiers' perceptions. The facts are that out of
that three thousand, only five hundred core protestors are
gathered around the bell. Perhaps a thousand others are listening to them and giving them encouragement, while another fifteen hundred spectators hang around the borders of
the Commons. It is difficult, maybe impossible, for the
guardsmen to make distinctions; all they see are thousands
of people, some of whom are shouting slogans and ringing
the bell.

At about this time, Brigadier General Canterbury declares

to his troops, "These students are going to have to find out what law and order is all about."

Allison Krause is crossing the Commons to meet up with Barry Levine. Earlier in the day, as ignorant as most of their classmates about the ban, they'd agreed to take part in the noon protest. Levine is standing atop the hill near Taylor Hall—it's called Blanket Hill—watching the demonstration and the armed soldiers standing some one hundred yards beyond. In a moment, he spots Krause, striding toward him, her hair pinned up, accentuating her prominent cheekbones. She looks jaunty in jeans and a tan safari jacket over a gray T-shirt with one word printed boldly across its front—Kennedy. It's from her high school, named for John F. Kennedy. She stops for a moment to exchange a few words with a friend and fellow activist, Jeffrey Miller, then continues on.

As she crosses the Commons, so intent on finding Levine that she seems not to notice the demonstrators or the guardsmen, Brigadier General Canterbury decides to disperse the crowd. A Kent State policeman makes the announcement through a bullhorn, but hardly anyone hears it. Krause does, however. Levine notices the urgency in her walk as she quickly climbs Blanket Hill to join him. She is smiling.

On the Commons, the police officer climbs into a jeep with several guardsmen and drives back and forth, calling through the bullhorn, "This assembly is unlawful! The crowd must disperse at this time! This is an order!" The announcement is repeated several times. It is heard, but it is not heeded. Each time, the demonstrators respond with chants of "Power to the people! Pigs off campus!" or "One, two, three, four, we don't want your fucking war!" Campus police plead, "For your own safety, all bystanders and innocent people, leave!" Some do, some don't. No less than the soldiers, the protestors are suffering from a separation between fact and perception. The fact is, the rally has been banned, but to their collective mind, the order is unreasonable and intolerable because the demonstration has been peaceful.

Now Canterbury gives a fateful order, telling his men to lock and load their weapons and clear the Commons. There is a ragged clattering as rifle bolts are pulled back and allowed to slide forward, plucking rounds from the clips into the chambers. The guardsmen advance, and as tear gas grenades burst, anger fans through the crowd. Some shout abusive words or throw stones or both, others pick up the smoking canisters and toss them back toward the soldiers. But in the end, they retreat, splintering into several groups, one of which scatters up Blanket Hill.

Canterbury orders a seventy-man detachment from G Troop of the 107th Cavalry to follow them. The soldiers' line of march takes them onto the practice football field, where they find themselves blocked by a chain-link fence that partially encloses the field. The detachment stands fast, apparently confused as to what they are to do next. A large group of students is massed in front of Taylor Hall, to the guardsmen's left, a smaller band is in the Prentice Hall parking lot a short distance away. A desultory, stationary battle takes place. Grenade launchers pop, canisters arc over the greensward and explode, the stench fouling the spring air. The students respond with their weapons—stones and bad language; a few again pick up the grenades and fling them back toward the soldiers. Perceptions and reality. Poorly trained, poorly led, worn out from days of suppressing first a trucker's strike and then seemingly endless flare-ups of campus unrest, their way partly barricaded by the chain-link fence, an angry mob in front of them, the guardsmen see themselves as trapped.

Krause is in the parking lot with Levine. Earlier, retreating up Blanket Hill, she had torn a moistened cloth she carried for protection against tear gas and gave half to a friend, a gesture that Levine thought demonstrated her unselfishness. As they moved up the hill, guardsmen screened by tear gas smoke advancing on them, Krause began to cry, and it wasn't from the gas. "Why are they doing this to us?" she asks Levine. "Why don't they let us be?"

Perceptions and reality. There was an innocence in her cry of the heart, but it ignored the reasons why the National Guard was called to Kent in the first place and could not "let them be." Krause had not taken part in the destruction that occurred over the weekend, but she was aware of it. In the name of protesting the actions of a remote federal government, vandals had lashed out at shopkeepers who had nothing even remotely to do with making war policy and wrecked businesses that had taken a lifetime to build. Arsonists had burned down a campus building and then assaulted the firemen whose duty it was to protect life and property, at risk of their own lives. The protests had turned into a mob riot that a small-town police force could not be expected to contain, and six policemen were in fact injured. This is not to say that the guardsmen were in any way justified in doing what they eventually did. God knows it is not to say that Krause, or any of the other victims, "deserved what they got." It is to say that the demonstrators who resorted to violence, the sort of blind, pointless violence that is not an expression of dissent so much as it is an emotional outburst, a kind of collective, destructive tantrum, also collaborated in the tragedy that would claim her life.

Krause's first reaction to the guard's disruption of the rally, sorrow rather than anger, gave way to rage when a tear gas canister landed next to her and Levine, bursting in their faces. Covering her face with her wet cloth, she ran, then turned and screamed at the troops. Levine pulled her along, fearing that the troops were getting too close. Twice more, she turned and yelled, as if she could stop the advance with her voice alone; twice more Levine had to pull her forward. Finally, with one hand holding the rag to her mouth, the other holding Levine's, she reached the parking lot.

Now she stands there with Levine and perhaps twenty other students, among whom are William Schroeder, some sixty feet behind her, and off to one side, fifty feet away, her and Levine's friend, Jeffrey Miller. They are all observing the detachment of soldiers in the practice field below, but Krause and Levine are not watching passively. They hurl epithets and stones—a symbolic gesture, as the guardsmen are a hundred or more yards away.

An officer, realizing the troops are confused, passes through the students clustered around Taylor Hall and walks down to the practice field to see what the problem is. Some guardsmen are seen huddling together, like a football team, several others kneel and point their weapons at the students, but do not fire. The menacing action convinces most of the students to leave. At this point, Brigadier General Canterbury considers that the crowd has been dispersed and passes the word to the guardsmen to return to the Commons. Assuming the action is over, the rest of the spectators at Taylor Hall drift off, clearing a path for the soldiers. They retrace their steps, with the band of students in the Prentice Hall lot jeering them as they leave. Walking beside them is a professional news photographer named John Darnell. G Troop reaches the crest of the hill. In a few moments, they will be able to clear a corner of Taylor Hall and return unimpeded to the Commons. It is then that Darnell sees a platoon of twenty-eight men turn around and march back a few steps. He ducks behind a column of Taylor, checking his camera's focus and f-stops, because the sun is in his eyes. The scene framed by his lens will become embedded in the American consciousness for years to come: soldiers in gas masks kneeling or standing as they aim their rifles at the students in the parking lot.

To freeze the image and look at it in retrospect, we can sense something almost mystical in this instant before the triggers are squeezed, a quality of the inevitable. It is as though what is about to happen needs to happen, a release of intolerable pressures. All the dark, diffuse, irrational forces that have been gathering in the country for years have come together here and now, on a May afternoon in the bright American heartland, to demand a blood sacrifice.

The four principal victims are on the altar, the parking lot. Let us freeze an image of them. Krause is facing the guardsmen, so is Miller. Schroeder, who has been a spectator, has turned partway around to leave. Scheuer, who hasn't even been an observer, is hurrying to a class with a friend. The paths that have brought them to this moment are as different as they are. We know something of Allison Krause, but what of Miller, Schroeder, and Scheuer?

In magazine profiles and in a docudrama about the Kent

State massacre, Schroeder was portrayed as a near super-
man, as if an idealized image were needed to emphasize how
pointless and unjustified his death was. It's easy to see why
the media was tempted to do this. Schroeder's biography almost reads like a press release for the all-American boy, a
Jack Armstrong come to life.

His path to the Prentice Hall lot began in Dillonvale, a
Cincinnati suburb, where he lived until he was four years
old, when the family moved to Lorain, Ohio. His childhood
hero was the Lone Ranger's sidekick, Tonto. Schroeder and
his brother and sister all had an interest in Indian lore,
which led the family to take tours of museums and historical sites. At one, Fort Ancient, near the town of Lebanon, he
followed a marked Indian trail and made an original discov-
ery of an arrowhead, which was verified as authentic by museum officials at the site. The arrowhead became one of his
most valued possessions. His find inspired him to buy a ge-
ologist's pick, and he spent family holidays rock collecting
and digging for artifacts.

He was an honor student in elementary school, joined the
Cub Scouts, started cornet lessons, was a member of the
Service Club, and was chosen to be captain of the safety patrol. He joined the Boy Scouts at age eleven, played in the
school orchestra, and was enrolled in the honors class in junior high school. He played in the band, as well as on the
basketball and football teams, and was elected to the student

council. At thirteen, he earned the last Boy Scout merit badge required for the rank of Eagle Scout by taking a long canoe trip with his troop through the boundary waters of Minnesota.

This impressive record continued in high school, where he played baritone horn in the varsity band, quit the band to play basketball, at which he excelled though at six feet he had to play against much taller opponents, ran cross-country, and was elected captain of the track team in his senior year. Inquisitive, studious, and intelligent, he graduated twenty-second out of a class of 453.

Pursuing his boyhood interest, he entered the Colorado School of Mines in 1969 to major in geology and minor in psychology. A bullet from a U.S. Army rifle, fired by an American soldier, would end his life in a year, but Schroeder went to college on an ROTC scholarship, granted to only nine hundred of the twelve thousand students who applied for it that year. His early fascination with Indian lore led him to study all the Indian wars, which in turn drew him to study the Civil War, the two World Wars, the Korean War, and, finally, the one he was likely to fight in, Vietnam. In accepting the scholarship, he'd signed away ten years of life, agreeing to take ROTC for four years of college, then to serve four more on active duty and another two in the Army Reserve. Schroeder's pace as a high achiever didn't slacken at the Colorado School of Mines: dean's list with a 3.1 grade point average; first place in military science class; intramural basketball team; Association of the United States Army award for excellence in history.

A real-life tragedy is the combination of blind circumstance and human folly, weakness, or ignorance that ends in death. Blind circumstance entered Schroeder's life during his first year at the School of Mines. The school stopped offering geology, substituting it with geological engineering, with an emphasis on mining. Cutbacks in the humanities department also removed psychology from the curriculum. He decided to transfer to Kent State and to change his major to psychology.

There he continued as before, racking up a 3.28 average, while working in a school cafeteria for wages and one free meal a day, then at a factory in town. He'd always paid his own way, earning enough in the summer between high school and college to buy a new Fiat, but his class schedule at Kent State became too demanding and he finally quit the part-time jobs, relying on his savings to meet daily expenses.

Two weeks before his death, he wrote to his sister, attending the University of Kansas: "Now that I am free all of the time, I am reading, walking, and generally having the real fun of being creative. I was loaned a $200 camera and all the film I can possibly ever use. Bruce (a classmate and cinematography major) and I take photography excursions and he is teaching me the ropes. I go to all the free lectures, concerts or bull sessions on campus. I'm finally getting some semblance of an education."

Schroeder was gregarious and made friends easily and also loved to travel. Despite a class and work schedule that would have crushed most undergraduates, he'd managed to visit the Grand Canyon, Florida, and New Mexico. On one of his journeys, his traveling companions were a Mennonite missionary and two young conscientious objectors who were doing service in an Army hospital. He got on well with them. Talking to them might have affected his outlook on the war—it's impossible to know if it did—but his plans for the future had begun to change. He thought that a trained psychologist might be as important on a battle front as a chaplain, and was considering going to graduate school before he went on active duty. Deeper questions were on his mind, and he'd discussed them with his roommate, Cusella. Nixon's escalation of the war into Cambodia troubled him. He wondered if he could continue in the ROTC program and go on to serve in the military so long as it was fighting in Vietnam.

Did these doubts and questions draw him toward the demonstration? That too is impossible to know. It's just as likely, perhaps more likely, that he was going about his ordinary business (if any business could have been ordinary during those tumultuous four days) and had stopped to watch out of curiosity.

The last message his parents, Louis and Florence Schroeder, received from him was a thank-you note in verse.

I am a child, I last awhile,
You can't perceive all the pleasure in my smile.
You make the rules, you say what's fair,
It's a lot of fun to have you there.
Thanks for the weekend, and every other weekend, and
*   every other day,*
And everything.

Sandy Scheuer's path begins in Germany, from where her parents, Martin and Sarah, emigrated to the United States. As Sarah told an interviewer, she and her husband wanted "to guarantee that our daughters would live in a country with freedom." The family settled in Youngstown, the smoky steel and manufacturing city forty miles east of Kent, near the Pennsylvania border. Sandy was a young woman with a long, graceful stride; her dark hair framed a face that a friend described as "angelic." Young men were enchanted by her aura of innocence, her compassion. After her death, one of them, Marty Levick, would write, "This is Sandy, a friend I will always remember and cherish till my life no longer is." Her steady boyfriend, an Ohio State fraternity man named Bruce Burkland, wrote a letter to the *Youngstown Vindicator*, recalling her capacity to "spread joy, happiness, and laughter in people's hearts wherever she went."

Levick took the last picture of Scheuer—it was to appear in *Time* magazine—showing her staring at the rubble of the ROTC building on Sunday. She was holding a stray dog by a leash made of ribbon. She and a couple of friends had adopted the dog, which was about to have puppies. On Saturday, she'd asked Levick if he could take the dog home with him because the end of the spring term was approaching and where were the animal and its pups to go? Levick declined—the dog was a bedraggled-looking creature, and he already had a dog and had no idea what he would do with puppies.

Scheuer felt sorry for stray animals and lonely people, and was willing to lend a hand to anyone in trouble. Her compassion was tempered by strict moral principles and opinions, which, in Levick's recollection, leaned toward "a disapproving negative approach." Presumably he meant she could be quick to censure what she considered bad behavior. She was majoring in speech and hearing therapy, and was no revolutionary firebrand. No kind of revolutionary whatsoever. The path that brought her to the Prentice Hall parking lot had nothing to do with the war or politics. She was simply crossing the lot on her way to a class.

Jeffrey Miller was different, a committed antiwar activist,

though that term must be understood within the context of Kent State. Like Krause, he advocated nonviolence, and was so far from the Weather Underground end of the spectrum that he'd called home in Plainfield, New York, to ask his mother, Elaine Holstein, if it was all right for him to attend Monday's rally. In a statement filed with lawyers during a wrongful death civil lawsuit in 1975, Mrs. Holstein (she'd remarried after her divorce from Miller's father) described her younger son as a boy "born with an extra portion of ideals and concern for people." At age six, spotting a broken bottle in the backyard, he'd said, "Somebody could get hurt," and picked up the bottle and nearly sliced off a finger. Two years later, she received a phone call from the editor of *Ebony* magazine congratulating her on her son. "He's going to be another Martin Luther King," the editor had said, explaining that Miller had called the magazine, declared that he was interested in civil rights, and wanted information about the plight of black Americans.

The Vietnam War was in its early stages while Miller was in high school. This was the period when most Americans believed victory was at hand, their illusions sustained by a steady diet of optimistic forecasts from the military and the White House, by Defense Secretary Robert McNamara's statistical pronouncements—so many enemy killed, so many villages pacified. Miller had a different take on the war, which he expressed in a poem written shortly before his sixteenth birthday. It wasn't the sort of poem the *New Yorker* would publish, but it showed that adolescents sometimes can be more perceptive than generals and secretaries of defense.

The strife and fighting continue into the night.
Mechanical birds sound of death as they buzz overhead,
spitting fire into the doomed towns where the women
and children run and hide in the bushes and ask why—
why are we not left to live our own lives?

In the pastures converted into battlefields
the small metal pellets speed through the air, pausing
*   occasionally to claim another victim.*
A teenager from a small Ohio farm clutches his side
in pain and as he feels his life ebbing away, he too asks
*   why—*
why is he dying here, thousands of miles from home,
giving his life for those who did not even ask his help?

The War Without a Purpose marches on relentlessly,
not stopping to mourn for its dead,
content to wait for its end.
But all the frightened parents who still have their sons
*   fear that*
the end is not in sight.

Two years later, Miller was a freshman at the University of Michigan, where his brother, Russ, was a senior. Russ had entered college in 1964, the year before the first U.S. combat troops were committed to Vietnam. Though he was only three years older than Jeffrey, he seemed to belong to a different generation, for the world had changed in those three years, and the college campuses of 1967 bore only a physical resemblance to those of 1964. Jeff Miller tried to live the undergraduate life of Russ Miller, joining his brother's fraternity in his sophomore year. Serenading under the windows of girls' dorms and sorority houses struck him as frivolous with a war going on. Some of his old high-school classmates had fought in Vietnam, and he was troubled by the change he saw in them when he returned home on vacations or semester breaks. After his brother graduated, he began to feel a bit lost and lonely, feelings aggravated by the breakup of his parents' marriage and the end of his relationship with a high-school sweetheart. In January 1970, he transferred to Kent State, to be with several of his friends from his hometown.

On the morning of May 4, he phoned his mother. She was aware of the disturbances on campus, and he wanted to assure her that he was all right. After making a bitter comment about President Nixon's characterization of anti-war protestors as "bums," he told her that a rally was going to be held at noon and that he was thinking of attending.

"Is that okay?" he asked. Mrs. Holstein replied that she had faith in his judgment but questioned if the rally would accomplish anything. He remarked that it probably couldn't, but he felt strongly about the war and the National Guard's occupation of the campus and wanted to take a stand.

Now he is taking that stand in the Prentice Hall lot near his friends Allison Krause and Barry Levine. They all three see the guardsmen wheel and aim their rifles. Photographer Darnell is behind the column of Taylor Hall, focusing his camera. He has marched with the soldiers across the practice field and up and down Blanket Hill, and at no time has he felt in danger. He is not expecting what happens next. He hears a shot, and then a volley, like the popping in a popcorn machine, only much louder. He snaps a picture, another and another.

Twenty of the twenty-eight guardsmen from G Troop fire into the air or the ground, but eight shoot directly at the students in the lot. Student photographer John Filo is there, also taking pictures. His first thought is that the guardsmen must be firing blanks, an illusion of which he is disabused when a halo of dust comes off a cement sculpture near him and a bullet chews bark off a tree. Filo drops his camera and flees down the hill. At about the same time, Jeffrey Miller, 270 feet from the guardsmen, is shot in the mouth and falls. Allison Krause, the girl who'd said that "flowers are better than bullets," is 330 feet away and takes a bullet in her left side. William Schroeder, 390 feet from the guardsmen, is shot in the left side of his back. Sandy Scheuer is also 390 feet away as a bullet pierces her neck.

They give their lives to the dark gods, and nine more give their blood. Except for one, all thirteen victims are chosen by a kind of random lottery, by the caprice of ballistics as rounds streak through the air at hypersonic speed, hitting some, missing others.

The exception is the student closest to the soldiers, Joseph Lewis, who is sixty feet away. The moment before the rifles crack, in a gesture of defiance, youthful bravado, and sheer craziness, eighteen-year-old Lewis gives the guardsmen the bird, and as he stands with his middle finger raised, a sergeant named Larry Schaefer aims and shoots him in the stomach.

Thomas Grace, about the same distance from the soldiers as Lewis, is struck in the ankle. John Cleary, one hundred feet away, is hit in the upper part of his chest. Alan Canfora, one of the protest leaders and Grace's roommate, ducks behind a tree as the firing begins, and is hit in the right wrist from a range of 225 feet. Dean Kahler, who had returned to campus from celebrating his twentieth birthday at home, is three hundred feet away when he is shot in the small of his back, a wound that will leave him paralyzed from the waist

down for the rest of his life. Douglas Wrentmore, the sophomore I'd interviewed the day after the shootings, is wounded
in the right knee from a distance of 330 feet. James Russell,
375 feet away, is struck in the right thigh. Robert Stamps,
almost five hundred feet from the line of fire, is wounded in
the right buttock. Donald MacKenzie is farthest from the
guardsmen at a distance of 750 feet when he takes a bullet
in the neck.

Sixty-seven rounds, thirteen seconds, thirteen casualties.

A few moments of utter, stunned silence follow the bar-
rage. Students stand frozen in mute disbelief. The scene re-
sembles a stopped-action film with the sound track turned
off. Then it is set back in motion, the sound goes up. The
guardsmen march away, seemingly indifferent to what they
have done. Screams of pain and cries for help echo across
the campus. Barry Levine, on both knees, cradles the dying
Allison Krause, and literally feels, in the blood trickling
through his fingers, her life slip away. John Filo, recovered
from his panic, has picked up the Nikkormat camera he
dropped. He sees Miller lying facedown on the pavement,
and the volume of blood flowing from his gaping head
wound is shocking—"as if someone had tipped over a
bucket," as Filo will describe it many years later. As he fo-
cuses his Nikkormat, Mary Vecchio, the teenage runaway,
runs into the frame, drops to one knee over the dead Miller,

and screams, "Oh, my God!" Filo snaps a picture, for which he will win a Pulitzer Prize. Six or seven guardsmen, led by a sergeant, come over to examine Miller's body. The sergeant rolls it over with his boot, which incenses the crowd of onlookers. The soldiers back away.

Alan Canfora's experiences in the aftermath can stand as typical of the pain and confusion suffered by all the survivors. As he lies behind the oak tree that has probably saved his life—it's been punctured by bullets—he feels the throbbing in his wrist and sees the blood pumping from the wound and thinks, "This is a nightmare but it's real! I've been shot!" He hears his roommate, Tom Grace, crying out that he has also been shot. Canfora knows this. A few seconds earlier, while rounds snapped overhead, Grace screamed when he was hit. He was trying to sit up to check the wound in his ankle, and Canfora yelled to him, "Stay down! Stay down! It's only buckshot!" In his shock, in his inability to comprehend that National Guardsmen would fire high-powered rifles into a crowd of unarmed students, Canfora had wrongly assumed that the soldiers were using shotguns. He runs to Grace and consoles him, then finds an uninjured friend, Jeff Hartzler, shows him his bloody arm, and says, "They shot me and Tom Grace too. He's over there. Go help him!" With police and ambulance sirens wailing in the background, Canfora goes into the Home Economics building, rinses his wound in a bathroom, wraps his wrist in a towel, and returns outside, where he flags down a car driven by a graduate student and his wife. He convinces them to take him to Robinson Memorial Hospital in Ravenna, six miles away. There, as he walks toward the emergency room, he looks inside the open rear door of a parked ambulance and sees Miller lying on a blood-smeared stretcher, a gaping wound disfiguring his face. Still under the misapprehension that buckshot had been fired, Canfora thinks that Miller is merely unconscious and wonders if plastic surgery will repair his face. Inside the hospital, he tries to calm Grace, who is calling for morphine to stop the pain. It is only after he has been treated that Canfora learns that rifles were the weapons and that several students have been killed. As he leaves the emergency room, he encounters Barry Levine and asks after Allison Krause, but is hustled outside by a county sheriff's deputy before Levine can tell him that she is among the dead.

In literary tragedies, the central figure is the tragic hero. In classical or Shakespearean drama, it is a flawed king or prince like Oedipus or Hamlet; in modern plays, it is an ordinary man like Willy Loman whose weaknesses lead to his downfall. There seldom are heroes in real life tragedies, only victims and perpetrators, but in the aftermath of the Kent State Massacre, one man does something heroic, a professor of geology named Glenn Frank. Recovered from their shock, students are enraged at the National Guard. The soldiers have retreated back to the Commons, only to face a large and hostile crowd. Several hundred sit down and demand to know why the guardsmen had shot their classmates. An officer replies, "Disperse or we will shoot again." The students do not move. Some appear ready to attack the soldiers. While he understands their fury, and to an extent shares in it, Frank knows that another confrontation will only compound the horror. He gathers several faculty marshals and persuades guard officers to allow them to speak with the demonstrators. Led by Frank, the marshals then plead with the students to return to their residences and avoid any rash actions. His and those of his fellow marshals are perhaps the sole voices of reason that day. Somehow, they keep the angry crowd in check, and after twenty minutes of begging, some of it quite emotional, they succeed in bringing the students to their senses. Frank openly weeps as they break up and leave the Commons. Without him and the faculty he had rallied to his side, many more lives would have been lost.

Chapter 3

The Kent State Massacre remains a unique event in American history—it was the first and only time American troops fired upon and killed American students. As I mentioned earlier, its closest historical parallel was the Boston Massacre of 1770. In some details, these two incidents bear an uncanny resemblance to each other; in other details, they diverge considerably. To compare them thoroughly, we have to take a look at what happened after the Kent State shootings and examine a few critical questions that are still unanswered—and at this late date are likely to remain so.

One question, however, can be answered. Were the shootings justified? No. Two major investigations of the massacre were conducted, one by the U.S. Department of Justice and one by the President's Commission on Campus Unrest, also called the Scranton Commission after its chairman, former Pennsylvania Gov. William Scranton. It will be recalled that at the press conference on May 5, Brigadier General Canterbury claimed that the guardsmen's lives were in danger: Lethal objects like bricks and slabs of concrete were being thrown at them. The lieutenant whom I interviewed the same day reiterated his commanding officer's tale, stating that some demonstrators were trying to wrest the soldiers' rifles from them. With a few variations, this was essentially the story told by the guardsmen involved in the shooting. Both the Justice Department and the Scranton Commission concluded that it was a total lie. The Justice Department stated that the distances between the students and the line of fire were such as to pose not even a remote danger to the soldiers.

Its summary goes on to say the following: "Only two (students) were shot from the front. Seven were shot from the side and four were shot from the rear. . . . The guardsmen were not surrounded. . . . They could have easily continued going in the direction which they had been going."

The Scranton Commission, while deploring the actions of some protestors in Kent and on campus on Friday, Saturday, and Sunday nights, concluded that the "indiscriminate firing of rifles into a crowd of students and the deaths that followed were unnecessary, unwarranted, and inexcusable."

Nevertheless, not one enlisted man or officer was ever convicted of any crime in connection with the shootings.

That brings us to the unanswered questions.

Was there an order to fire?

In his interview with me, the lieutenant had said the soldiers fired without orders. In the criminal and civil trials that followed the incident, guardsmen and officers alike testified to the same effect. Testimony from eyewitnesses was conflicting. Some stated they had heard a command; others that a sergeant or officer had discharged his pistol, signaling the men to fire. The closest anyone has come to resolving this question is William A. Gordon, a journalist whose 1990 book, *The Fourth of May: Killings and Coverups at Kent State*, is regarded as one of the few definitive and accurate accounts of the massacre. After examining secret federal grand jury testimony and FBI interviews with eyewitnesses, Gordon surmises that there was an order. Two key witnesses—former Marines who'd seen action in Vietnam—told investigators that they'd seen a sergeant give a hand signal to fire. Others stated that a major gave the signal with a baton or riot stick. Both officers denied under oath giving any such order, and guardsmen further testified that a hand signal to fire did not exist (in fact, it did—the U.S. Army teaches a whole series of hand-and-arm signals in basic training).

Regardless of who gave the order, if one was given, the movements of the guardsmen were too coordinated to have been the spontaneous action of stressed-out, trigger-happy soldiers. Twenty-eight men had turned as one, marched a few yards, formed a skirmish line, then fired almost in unison. This raises another question, assuming they were not responding to direct orders: Did they conspire among themselves to shoot? The evidence suggesting they did was the huddle some went into minutes before the firing began. Gordon concludes that there was no conspiracy, but other journalists and authors who investigated the incident believe there was. One was James Michener. His 559-page book, *Kent State: What Happened and Why*, was among the first major examinations of the massacre. Michener stops short of accusing the guardsmen of outright conspiracy, but opines that they'd reached some sort of rough agreement to open fire while they conferred near Taylor Hall.

Who started the fire in the ROTC building, and why did the Kent State University police make no attempts to arrest the arsonists, disperse the crowd, or protect the firemen from the mob that attacked them when they arrived to fight the blaze?

These are key questions for at least one reason:

Although the decision to call in the National Guard was made at 5:00 p.m. on Saturday, May 2, the guard did not arrive until 10:00 p.m. on Sunday, by which time the building was engulfed in flames. The fire was what prompted the authorities to deploy guardsmen on the campus. In other words, if there had been no fire there would have been no soldiers on KSU grounds and no one would have been killed on Monday.

Absent hard facts as to who caused the fire, we can only fall back on plausible hypotheses. There are two:

- The incendiaries were student radicals from Kent State, elsewhere, or both.

- They were *agents provocateur* assigned to incite violence as part of a government plot to smash the antiwar movement once and for all.

To further confuse matters, both hypotheses are plausible. Supporting the first (which I adhere to, albeit with reservations) are the reports of non–Kent State students observed in town and on campus during the three days of disturbances preceding the shootings. I don't think they were part of any organized protest, as Mayor Satrom suggested when he said that "carloads" of antiwar militants were descending on Kent, and as Governor Rhodes stated when he blamed the disturbances on "outside agitators." To say that implies that the antiwar movement was far more coherent and cohesive than it was, capable of dispatching "flying squads" to likely hot spots to stir up trouble. The strange faces probably belonged to students from Akron and Ohio State University, who frequented Kent. There was, however, a core of SDS members at Kent State, students who, in Prof. Glenn

Frank's words, "espoused Maoist doctrine and hostility that went well beyond reasonable concern for Vietnam and Cambodia." Also, destroying targets like ROTC buildings was part of the Weather Underground's program of "exemplary violence." Further evidence that the culprits were local is the fact that reliable witnesses saw Kent State students throwing matches through the windows of the building, although these attempts appeared to have been ineffectual at first. Finally, after the blaze was well underway, there was the stoning of Kent firemen and the slashing of fire hoses by people in the surrounding crowd. In my opinion, this suggests that the arson was the work of protesters. It strains credibility to assume that the government, on such short notice, could deploy a sufficient number of operatives to start the blaze and prevent the firemen from fighting it.

Supporting the second hypothesis is the baffling inaction of the KSU police. Not only did they stand by while the arsonists torched the building and the mob attacked the firemen, they apparently had advance warning of what was going to happen. One officer even told investigators that he'd advised a TV camera crew not to pack their cameras because "we are going to have a fire tonight."

Author William Gordon, in his examination of FBI files and grand jury testimony, uncovered a startling fact. A high school student named George Walter Harrington admitted to federal investigators that he'd had a hand in starting the fire, but he was never prosecuted and was never identified until years after the event. Why?

A private citizen named Peter Davies was perhaps the staunchest advocate of the theory that Kent State was a part of a government conspiracy. An insurance salesman who'd emigrated to the United States from England, Davies was shocked that such an incident could occur in his adopted country. Realizing it could have been his children on the KSU campus, he launched a personal campaign to obtain justice. His inquiries into the massacre led to a book, *The Truth About Kent State*, to numerous essays in the *New York Times*, the *Village Voice*, and other publications, and to a forty-page report he submitted to a subcommittee of the House Judiciary Committee investigating the incident.

Davies wrote an essay describing his experiences with the subcommittee entitled "The Kent State Sting." In it, he flatly states that the Nixon administration killed the congressional investigation to cover up the government's role in what happened at Kent State. That role, he continues, was the employment of *agents provocateur* to burn down the ROTC building and incite a student riot.

In October 1970, he says, "The Justice Department contacted Ohio's special prosecutor, Robert Balyeat, and asked him to furnish the names of all those likely to be indicted by

the Portage County grand jury. Although local law prohibited the disclosure of such information to anyone, county
judge Edwin Jones violated the law by approving the request. Significantly, the names of six men targeted for indictment in connection with the burning of the ROTC
building, which appeared on three lists sent to Washington,
subsequently were not indicted. Apparently the Justice Department, to protect its own involvement, had struck the six
names. If what had happened at Kent State was just the local incident that it was claimed to be, why was Washington
so interested in the names of those likely to be prosecuted?"

Davies then presents a detailed summary of how the
Nixon administration, through complex maneuvers that
amounted to an obstruction of justice as egregious as that in
the Watergate scandal, quashed the congressional investigation (which was chaired by a Democrat, Rep. Don Edwards
of California). The end result was a federal grand jury probe
that culminated, on March 29, 1974, in the indictments of
the eight National Guardsmen believed to have shot directly
into the crowd. Five of the eight were accused of killing the
four students. The defendants were not indicted for murder
or attempted murder, however, but for criminal violations
of the victims' civil rights. They included Sergeant Larry
Schaefer, who'd admitted to FBI investigators that he had
deliberately shot Joseph Lewis, the eighteen-year-old freshman who'd made an obscene gesture. (Schaefer repeated his

admission in a newspaper interview ten years after the event, claiming that Lewis's free hand was behind his back, causing Schaefer to think that he had a weapon.)

Davies alleges that the trial, which began in the fall of 1974, was a farce. The government's chief prosecutor, to cite one example, undermined his own case by conceding in his opening statement that the government had no ballistics evidence to prove which soldier had shot which student. In so many words, the government was admitting that it wasn't sure if the five men indicted for the deaths of Krause, Miller, Scheuer, and Schroeder were in fact the five who had fired the fatal shots. In general, the prosecution's case was so poorly prepared (and Davies suggests this was deliberate) that the judge stopped the trial, dismissed the jury, and acquitted all eight guardsmen. Thus, Davies concludes, the soldiers were protected from further prosecution under the law of double jeopardy, and the cover-up of the government's covert role in what happened at Kent State was preserved.

For the record, several key Nixon aides, long after they had broken with the administration over Watergate and no longer had a reason to protect the president, the attorney general, FBI director J. Edgar Hoover, or any other high official, denied that Washington had a plan to crush antiwar dissent. In the archives of the May 4 Resource Center at Kent State there is a 1980 interview with former White House counsel John Dean. In it, Dean states that he had no knowledge of a White House or Justice Department campaign to quell antiwar ferment. Asked if Kent State had been engineered as a show of force to intimidate dissidents, Dean replied, "I never had the impression that Kent State was orchestrated by the administration."

So Davies may have added two and two and come up with five, but the intriguing questions he poses—Why was the Justice Department interested in knowing the names of persons who might be charged with starting the fire? Why did Nixon's White House go to such lengths to stop the congressional investigation?—have never been answered. Given the paranoia, lawlessness, and conspiratorial behavior that characterized that administration, it's still possible that someone in the future will unearth classified documents showing that the Kent State Massacre resulted from a concerted government effort to smash domestic dissent by provoking incidents of deadly violence. In so many words, the shootings may have been an act of calculated murder instigated by men in very high places.

Justice, as will be seen, was carried out with more efficiency, and perhaps more fairness, in the wake of the Boston Massacre two hundred years earlier. As a schoolboy in the 1950s, like every other American kid at the time, I had been taught that the massacre was the unprovoked shooting of innocent citizens by the brutal soldiery of an imperial power led by a tyrannical king. An examination of the facts shows that it wasn't quite that way. Like Kent State, the incident was controversial and open to different interpretations of what happened, who did what, and why.

One other parallel, no doubt coincidental, was that both massacres occurred on a Monday, after a weekend of minor clashes. A more relevant similarity can be drawn between the atmospheres in the American colonies in the late 1760s and early 1770s and in the America of the late 1960s and early 1970s. In the latter, tension was caused by what Jacques Barzun, in his monumental study of western civilization, *From Dawn to Decadence*, calls The Revolt of Youth against the authority of the U.S. government to wage an undeclared foreign war, which grew into a revolt against almost all forms of authority—the church, the university, business, traditional morals. In the former, the cause of disaccord were restive subjects chafing against the power of the British government to levy duties on imported goods, impose arbitrary taxes, and quarter armies in the towns and cities of the thirteen North American colonies.

Of them all, Massachusetts was the most restive, and the heart of anti-British sentiment was Boston. We think of that city today as the Athens of America for its many prestigious universities and its cultural institutions. It has also been associated with blue-blood gentility and staid social mores, but in the mid-eighteenth century it was a colonial outpost and seaport of some fifteen thousand people with a reputation for rowdiness and what was then considered radical politics. Among its more prominent agitators and propagandists were a silversmith and engraver named Paul Revere and a lawyer named John Adams.

Troubles began with the British Parliament's passage of the Stamp Act in 1765, which placed taxes on colonial commercial and legal documents, newspapers, pamphlets, almanacs, and other periodicals. The purpose was to raise money for defense expenditures; Great Britain's victory in the French and Indian War two years earlier had increased the government's military burden, requiring it to maintain military garrisons to protect frontier settlements in the colonies. A Stamp Act had been passed in England in 1712 and was a common means of generating revenue there, but its imposition in North America immediately brought a tidal wave of protest. Objecting to Parliament's direct taxation and insisting on their rights as British citizens to be taxed only through their own representatives—the constituent assemblies that had made the colonies largely self-governing for over a century—colonists neutralized the Stamp Act by refusing to use the stamps, by burning them, by intimidating stamp distributors, and when all else failed, by rioting. North American merchants retaliated by agreeing not to import manufactured goods from England.

In October 1765, the assemblies of nine colonies convened in New York, drew up resolutions of rights and grievances, and petitioned the Crown and Parliament to repeal the measure. This was done, largely under pressure from British merchants and factory owners, whose exports to the colonies had suffered as a result of the boycott. The government, however, still needed to pay for its military forces in America. How could this be done without offending the colonists while at the same time affirming Parliament's right of colonial authority? Charles Townshend, King George III's finance minister, proposed a series of four acts, which were passed by Parliament between June 15 and July 2, 1767.

The colonists, however, were mightily offended by the Townshend Acts, as they came to be known. Among other things, these measures levied an import tax on glass, paint, paper, lead, and tea, suspended the New York assembly until it met its financial obligations for the expenses of British troops stationed there, and established strict and often arbitrary methods of collecting customs duties, which included additional customs officers, spies, coast guard vessels, search warrants, and a Board of Customs Commissioners, located in Boston.

The practice of taxation through representative assemblies was once again threatened. Colonists resisted with fiery speeches, deliberate evasions of customs duties, a renewal among merchants of the boycott on British imports, and acts of physical violence against the Crown's enforcement agents, especially in Boston.

The Board of Commissioners, intimidated by the resistance and desiring to put Boston's many malcontents in their place, demanded military protection. The commander in chief of the British army in North America, Gen. Thomas Gage, agreed and ordered two infantry regiments to be withdrawn from Nova Scotia and sent to Boston. They landed in October 1768. Two more regiments and part of a third arrived from Ireland six weeks later. In all, nearly four thousand troops, roughly one soldier for every four citizens, were stationed in the city. The townspeople were outraged. They viewed the British troops in the same way the students at Kent State viewed the Ohio National Guard—as an oppressive army of occupation.

Unlike the National Guardsmen, the redcoats were professional soldiers, many of them drawn from the dregs of society. Although Americans had fought alongside them in the French and Indian War, they did not like the Lobster Backs, regarding them, not without reason, as surly, brutal, insolent, greedy, and licentious. One regiment, the 29th Worcestershire, camped on Boston Common, and the stench from latrines blew through the city with every little breeze.

That, however, was not as objectionable as the attempt to quarter the other regiments in Boston homes. This wasn't tried because barracks space was lacking; placing troops under the roofs of Boston's agitators, the government hoped, would intimidate them. No Boston man with a wife and daughters could tolerate the presence of British soldiers in his house. The city council took a firm stand, declaring that citizens would not be required to furnish living quarters for army personnel until all other available space was filled. Eventually, the governor of Massachusetts gave in and housed the troops in several empty factory buildings.

For the next eighteen months, townspeople and troops abraded one another. One source of friction was the posting of sentries at all public buildings; these guards were vivid reminders that Boston was an occupied city and heightened the feeling among the populace that it had been invaded. Boston newspapers and polemicists (among them, John Adams's older cousin Samuel Adams) fanned resentment by publishing accounts of British "atrocities" against civilians. Although their officers tried to prevent trouble, the soldiers did in fact behave arrogantly and brawled with local men on the streets. They were, however, often provoked by Boston's rougher elements, who made a sport of taunting, tormenting, and picking fights with British soldiers.

By the winter of 1770, the mood in the city was as venomous and angry as the mood on American campuses two hundred years later. Things came to a head on the weekend of March 3 and 4. Boston youths fought with soldiers, cursed, harassed, and generally tried to prevent them from performing their duties. These outbursts were not planned, but were the spontaneous eruption of months of seething antagonism.

Monday, March 5, was cold and overcast; snow covered the cobblestone streets. A young barber's apprentice, Edward Garrick, had taken time off from his work to engage in the day's sport. He approached Hugh White, a 29th Regiment soldier on sentry duty at the Customs House on King Street, and insulted him. White had had enough and clubbed Garrick on the ear with the butt of his musket, knocking him down. Yelling for help, Garrick ran off, gathered a gang of young men, and returned to the Customs House. Pointing at White, he shouted, "There is the son of a bitch who knocked me down!" Someone dashed into a nearby church and began ringing the bell, which drew more people into the street (and we hear that bell, echoing through the centuries, when the Kent State protestors struck the victory bell to summon their compatriots to the rally). White now found himself facing an angry mob. Standing his ground, he called for the main guard. Led by a corporal, six men responded, and were soon joined by the duty officer, one Captain John Preston. The soldiers were at fixed bayonets, but their muskets were unloaded. Pushing through the crowd, crying out "Make way!" they came to White's relief.

By most accounts, Preston attempted to calm the crowd but was unsuccessful. The mob swelled to four hundred, and here the Boston Massacre differs from Kent State. The

Bostonians were better armed than the KSU students, with cudgels, staves, and even a few cutlasses. They were also much closer to the soldiers, a matter of a few yards at most, and were more belligerent and provocative. When the captain ordered his men to load their weapons, some townsmen began to yell, "Come on, you rascals, you bloody backs, you lobster scoundrels, fire if you dare! Goddamn you! Fire and be damned, we know you dare not!" All the while, they pelted the soldiers with snowballs and chunks of ice. Led by a tall, powerfully built mulatto from Framingham, Massachusetts, Crispus Attucks, they surged to within inches of the squad's bayonets, continuing to dare them to shoot.

Eyewitness accounts of what happened next conflict. This is how the *Boston Gazette and Country Journal* described the events in its edition of March 12, 1770:

> On this, the Captain commanded them to fire; and more snowballs coming, he again said, "Damn you, fire, be the consequence what it will!" One soldier then fired, and a townsman with a cudgel struck him over the hands with such force that he dropped his firelock; and rushing forward, aimed a blow at the Captain's head which grazed his hat and fell pretty heavy upon his arm. However, the soldiers continued the fire successively till seven or eight or, as some say, eleven guns were discharged.

Obviously seven, eight, or eleven guns could not have been fired by six men. It was later determined that several more men had shot from inside the Customs House.

For accuracy, most historians rely on the court testimony offered at the trial of Preston and the soldiers. The chain of events appeared to have been this: Responding to the townsmen's chants of "Fire and be damned," Preston told his men to hold their fire. Then someone in the crowd hurled a club, which struck Private Hugh Montgomery and knocked him off his feet. He stood up, aimed into the crowd, and fired. With all the commotion, the other soldiers probably had not heard Preston's order, given only moments before. When Montgomery discharged his musket, they probably assumed a command to fire had been given and discharged theirs at point-blank range. Apparently, the men inside the Customs House fired at about the same time, which accounts for the number of casualties: three killed outright, two mortally wounded, and six more wounded but not fatally.

Attucks, in the forefront, was killed instantly by two musket balls, one penetrating a lung, the other his liver.

Also killed on the spot was a sailor, James Caldwell, shot twice in the back, and Samuel Gray, shot in the head. A fourth man, a seventeen-year-old apprentice ivory-turner named Samuel Maverick, was shot through the stomach and died the next morning. The fifth fatality was Patrick Carr, a thirty-year-old leather worker, who later died of his wound, a ball that entered near his hip and came out the other side.

The six wounded were Christopher Monk, John Clark, Edward Payne, John Green, Robert Patterson, and David Parker.

As the smoke cleared, the crowd quickly fled and the soldiers returned to their barracks.

In contrast to what happened after the Kent State shootings, Captain Preston, the six soldiers, and four men alleged to have fired from the Customs House were promptly arrested, indicted for murder, and imprisoned pending trial by the Massachusetts Superior Court, which postponed the trial till the fall to give the citizens of Boston and its immediate vicinity time to calm down. To further dampen passions, the British regiments were withdrawn from the city.

Despite the outrage aroused by what the newspapers of the day termed a "bloody massacre" and "an inhuman tragedy," colonists remained coolheaded. At any rate, there was no rioting in the streets, or any additional acts of violence. Hundreds attended the funerals of the five slain men, held on Thursday, March 8. A dignified procession marched behind the hearses, while church bells pealed throughout Boston and in neighboring towns. Attucks, Caldwell, Carr, Gray, and Maverick were buried in a single vault. A commemorative marker, which exists to this day, was placed on their grave.

At the trials, Preston and the other accused were defended by John Adams, Josiah Quincy, Robert Auchmuty, and Sampson Blowers. The choice of Adams and Quincy was a curious one, as they were known leaders of dissent. Some historians speculate that they were picked because the jury was stacked in favor of the accused; choosing two radical lawyers to defend them would lend credibility to a verdict of acquittal. A second theory was that the jury was packed in the opposite direction and that with Adams and Quincy representing them, the defendants were insured a fair trial.

Preston testified that he gave no order to fire, that a soldier shot on his own volition after he was hit with a club, that the other soldiers fired in response to the townsmen's attack, and that he reprimanded his men for firing into the crowd without orders. His testimony was supported by numerous eyewitnesses. Several prosecution witnesses disputed his claim. They included the soldier whose butt stroke had started the whole thing, Hugh White, who testified that he heard an order to fire.

In the end, the jury found Preston and four men not guilty. Two other soldiers were convicted of manslaughter, but were released after being branded on their hands—a common punishment at the time. For three reasons, it is easy to see why the jury acquitted Preston and the others, much easier than in the cases of the eight guardsmen at Kent State. One: a number of impartial witnesses who were close to the captain swore that they heard no order to fire. Two: in the confusion, with the crowd hurling clubs and snowballs and shouting at them to shoot, the soldiers probably believed they'd heard a command to shoot. Three: the squad had been physically attacked by a mob at close quarters.

Although colonists reacted to the outcome with calm, they regarded it as proof of Britain's tyranny, and leaders of colonial rebellion were able to use it as such, as the antiwar movement used the acquittals of the guardsmen to show there was a government conspiracy to stifle dissent. It's possible that John Adams and Josiah Quincy had agreed to represent Preston and the soldiers because they knew the prosecution's case was weak and that an acquittal would have the effect it did. In furtherance of the incident's propaganda value, Paul Revere struck a famous engraving that he entitled "The Bloody Massacre on King Street." It was to the Boston incident what Filo's photo was to Kent State.

Among the differences between these two events was the public's attitude toward the victims. The five dead in Boston were hailed as heroes and martyrs to the cause of American liberty. Down to the present day, Crispus Attucks is a revered figure among African-Americans. It is true that the four dead in Ohio were regarded in much the same light by college students and those in the antiwar movement. The Kent State Massacre sparked the only massive student strike in U.S. history, with four million students shutting down eight hundred campuses across the country. In Maryland, young demonstrators closed U.S. Highway 1 outside Washington, D.C., while in the capital, thousands surrounded the White House. Students in San Francisco stormed city hall, calling for Nixon's impeachment. Unfortunately, the bomb-and-arson crowd got in the act, burning down some thirty ROTC buildings in protest.

But this huge and impassioned show of solidarity was deceptive. In the country at large, few sympathized with the victims or their families. In a nationwide poll conducted after the incident, 58 percent of Americans responded that the guardsmen had done the right thing; a mere 12 percent thought the shootings were unjustified. As author William Gordon remarked in his book, the killings were "the most popular murders ever committed in the United States."

That was no hyperbole. On October 16, 1970, an Ohio grand jury, impaneled three months earlier, exonerated the guardsmen and indicted twenty-five students for various offenses that occurred on campus and in the town of Kent prior to the shootings. The state prosecutor told a newsman that he thought the soldiers should have shot more students.

In one form or another, that lovely sentiment was expressed by private citizens, a few of whom took the trouble to write to the families of the dead. The rancor, venom, and sheer meanness of these communications showed that the dark gods of hate had not been satiated by the blood sacrifice. The archives of the May 4 Resource Center contain copies of three letters received by Louis and Florence Schroeder. They are reprinted below in full, with grammatical and punctuation errors left in and the senders' names deleted. In reading them, keep in mind that William Schroeder was in ROTC and on the dean's list and that his only crime was to have stopped to observe the rally.

Mr. And Mrs. Schroeder,

There's nothing better than a dead, destructive, riot making communist, and that's what your son was, if not he would have stayed away like a good American would do. Now you know what a goody-goody son you had. They should all be shot, then we'd have a better U.S.A. to live in. Be thankful he is gone. Just another communist.

Mrs. Schroeder,

I heard you on T.V. and if I were a policeman I would kill a lot more of these kids. Keep your kids at home then they do not get in trouble. My boys and girls do not get in trouble. Sure looks bad for you parents. Kids belong in Your home, entertain them in your home like we do here. hope the police and Army kill a lot more kids. It has to be stopped now as it is getting so you cannot go out on the street. We do not feel sorry for none of you parents. Keep your kids at home.

Dear Mrs. Schroeder,

I've just finished reading an associated press dispatch regarding the findings of a grand jury who found those four soldier murderers (as you consider them to be innocent). Madam—they were only doing their duty— perhaps some of them may have been just recently finished with high school or of college age themselves. Do you think they relished firing that live ammunition? Surely you must be aware that all national guard units were given official riots and mob violence training. They may not have received official orders; perhaps they only wanted to fire at the feet of that violent mob coming at them. Verbal abuse hurled at one is much different than when it is being chanted singily by a large wild mob of humans coming at you when the sight of the uniform of the law and order of this land was not enough to deter these misguided boys and girls from advancing—the law of self-preservation turns over. I have a son myself of college age. He made top seventeen percent in the national S.A.T. test for college. Where is he now? In Vietnam putting his life on the line that your children and other kids could sit back and have the fun of playing at war without the players. He did not want to be drafted—he wants to go to college so he took a four year hitch in the service of his choice—the Air Force—to sort of have some extra insurance by giving two more years of his youth to his country in insure his chance of having a start at an education through the G.I. Bill. Though your child may have been innocent of any wrong motives for being in that crowd of violence she [the writer was apparently confused about the sex of the Schroeders' child] was sure that they would send someone out to quell that mob from wonton distruction. She chose to be front of the actions. I am enclosing a copy of an article that has helped me considerable to understand myself and in tern to understand the why of some of the things my own son did. I am also enclosing an address where you may send twenty five cents for three free copies explaining who and what is really in back of the campus insurrection. Perhaps then, Mrs. Schroeder, you may realize that perhaps it was better for your child to lose his life now than end up entangled in a mesh of filth that has but one aim—to distroying freedom and education as we once enjoyed it in this country. I shall say another prayer for your child. May God help you to find love of soul in all this."

The Schroeder, Krause, Miller, and Scheuer families suffered further torments during the federal trial, listening to prosecutors portray their children as rabid subversives. In 1975, a wrongful death and injury trial opened, providing the first opportunity—five years after the shootings—to hear all the evidence. After three months of conflicting testimony, controversy over rulings excluding and including certain evidence, and charges of jury tampering, the jury decided not to award damages to the families of the dead and wounded. Two years later, the Sixth Circuit Court of Appeals in Cincinnati overturned that decision on the grounds that the judge, Donald Young, had mishandled the incident involving an alleged attempt to coerce a juror. A second civil trial began in December 1978, and in January 1979, the plaintiffs, financially and emotionally exhausted, settled out of court. The state of Ohio awarded them $675,000 in damages, to be split thirteen ways, and ordered the defendants—the National Guardsmen—to sign a statement of regret. While some of the families considered the three-paragraph statement to be an apology, words like "apologize" and "sorry" do not appear in it.

That ended the tragedy of May 4, 1970, except in the minds and souls of Louis and Florence Schroeder, Martin and Sarah Scheuer, Arthur and Doris Krause, Elaine Holstein and Bernie Miller, and in the minds and souls of the nine wounded who in the searing impact of .30 caliber bullets felt death touch them that afternoon.

And what about the tragedy's authors? In 1980, Glenn Frank, the geology professor and faculty marshal credited with preventing further bloodshed, wrote a letter to an Ohio eighth grader who was working on a social studies project and had asked him for his thoughts and feelings about the event.

"It is not at all curious that both extremes in this event firmly, and almost religiously, believe that they have moral justice and righteous power supporting their particular perceptions," Frank stated in his careful, balanced reply. "To most people there is no middle ground in this event. Most have a mind-set that will not allow any understanding of an opposite view or acceptance of even partial responsibility. . . . Why was Governor Rhodes so hostile with his 'brown shirts' comments? Why were students whom I knew espousing Maoist doctrine and hostility that went well beyond reasonable concern for Vietnam and Cambodia? . . . Everyone was at fault. The governor and the National Guard have not enhanced themselves in my eye by denying any responsibility, but neither have the students, radicals, and others who were directly involved or who defended the protestors by not assuming some degree of responsibility."

A tragedy, whether it is a work of literary art or a real-life event, requires the cooperation of fate (or circumstance) with human will and actions. While Frank's struggle to find a middle ground is admirable, to say that everyone was at fault is to say that no one was at fault. Overspreading the blame, he dilutes it to the point that the element of human agency is removed and thus transforms the Kent State Massacre into an act of God, a kind of natural disaster.

Yes, there was blame enough to share, but it cannot be shared equally. The militants who burned the ROTC building (assuming they and not *agents provocateur* were the culprits) can claim a measure of credit. So can those who committed mindless acts of vandalism in Kent on Friday night, and those who phoned threats to town merchants, and those who incited the protestors to throw stones and hurl verbal abuse at the guardsmen. Franks was right to criticize them for failing to admit some degree of responsibility. Like so many other activists during that time, they seemed to operate under the assumption that their cause was so manifestly righteous that any attempt to stop their actions, even when those actions resulted in mayhem, was unjustifiable repression.

The more extreme factions of the antiwar movement, like the Weathermen, can also be added to the long list of the tragedy's authors; their acts of nihilistic violence and intemperate rhetoric helped to create a fearful climate in the country. Jerry Rubin, not a Weatherman but a prominent activist, spoke at Kent State prior to the May demonstrations. He urged students to obtain weapons and "kill your parents." Virtually everyone in the audience dismissed him as a nut, but his words caused a great deal of anxiety in and around Kent.

But some high government officials also engaged in polarizing bombast, so their names should be included under Kent State's byline. Speaking of student dissenters on April 7, 1970—just three weeks before the shootings—then governor of California Ronald Reagan said, "If it takes a bloodbath, let's get it over with. No more appeasement." That same month, Vice President Spiro Agnew advised police and university administrators to "just imagine they [student protestors who throw rocks and make demands] are wearing brown shirts or white sheets and act accordingly." Apparently, Governor Rhodes plagiarized Agnew in the comments he made on May 3.

All of the above were contributing writers. The principal authors, whose names should appear in bold capital letters, were the guardsmen whose bullets killed or injured the thirteen victims. Because justice was so miscarried, we cannot say, and probably never will be able to say, exactly who they were, except for Sgt. Larry Schaefer. If an order to fire was given, the name of the officer or noncommissioned officer who gave it should appear above theirs.

". . . The king himself hath a heavy reckoning to make,

when all those legs and arms and heads, chopped off in a battle, shall join together at the latter day and cry all, 'We died at such a place,' " Shakespeare writes in *Henry V.* Those in power have an obligation to use their power wisely; the greater the power, the greater the obligation, and thus the greater is the fault for dereliction of that duty. By that standard, then, top billing should go to Ohio's Gov. James Rhodes and National Guard commanders Sylvester Del Corso and Robert Canterbury.

There was a bloody coda to the Kent State massacre. Just ten days later, two young students, one an innocent bystander, were shot by police during a protest at Jackson State University, a small, black teacher's college in Jackson, Mississippi. This was not an antiwar demonstration. It had been called because of racial incidents between the students and an all-white suburb near the campus. It turned into a mini-riot, with incidents of rock- and bottle-throwing, and the ROTC building was set on fire. City and state police responded. After the fire was put out, some one hundred officers armed with submachine guns, shotguns, and service revolvers marched with weapons drawn toward a campus dormitory. A roughly equal number of students were massed in front of the dorm. Someone either threw a bottle or dropped it. It struck the pavement with a loud noise.

According to some accounts, the police advanced on the crowd, then one of three things happened: a hand holding a pistol was seen in a dormitory window, a student actually fired a revolver from the window, or the police opened fire immediately after the bottle shattered. The only undisputed fact was that the law enforcement officers did shoot— pouring about 460 rounds into the building in a thirty-second fusillade. Philip Gibbs, a twenty-one-year-old senior with a wife and child, was killed by four bullets—two in the head, one under his left eye, and another in his left armpit. A seventeen-year-old high-school student, James Earl Green, was mortally wounded by a single gunshot wound as he was walking home from work at a grocery store.

The aftermath copied Kent State's. A grand jury refused to indict any of the officers involved, a civil jury found them not liable for any punitive damages, and in 1974 a U.S. Court of Appeals, while ruling that the police had overreacted, upheld the decision that they were not culpable in the two deaths.

Once again, the forces of authority had gotten away with murder. You can understand why college students in those days had begun to wonder if open season had been declared on them.

Chapter 4

The Boston Massacre was a turning point in American history. The shots fired by British soldiers on King Street in March 1770 led directly to the shots fired by the minutemen on Lexington Green in April 1775. Was the Kent State Massacre such a turning point? Did it have an enduring historical impact? Tucked away inside those questions is another, more poignant one: Did the four dead die for something or for no reason?

When I returned to the campus in the fall of 2004, I asked that of Mike Klesta, the managing editor of the KSU newspaper, the *Kent Stater*. A slender, fair-haired twenty-one-year-old, Klesta gave me an ironic, almost weary smile and frankly told me that he and most of his classmates were sick of hearing about May 4.

"Mention that you're from KSU, and people start to sing, 'Four Dead in Ohio,'" he said, sitting in the newspaper's offices on the ground floor of Taylor Hall. "Our basketball team made the elite eight in the NCAA playoffs two years ago, we have one of the best architecture schools in the country, but our claim to fame is May Fourth." He thought for a while. "They didn't die in vain. If it had been forgotten, they would have, but we have classes about May Fourth and there's a center here for studying conflict resolution that grew out of that. May Fourth changed views across the nation. The war had come home. No, they didn't die in vain."

The center Klesta referred to is the Center for Applied Conflict Management, which offers courses on nonviolent conflict resolution. Two experts on the incident, Dr. Thomas Hensley, a professor of political science at Kent State, and Dr. Jerry M. Lewis, a sociology professor who served as faculty marshal during the disturbances, point out that National Guard units and law enforcement officials established new guidelines for dealing with civil unrest in the wake of the tragedy.

"[They] have issued a caution to their troops to be careful because 'We don't want another Kent State,'" Hensley and Lewis stated in a paper they coauthored. "Insofar as this happened, lessons have been learned, and the deaths of the four young Kent State students have not been in vain."

They have a point, borne out by the antiwar demonstrations that took place in 2003, before the United States invaded Iraq. Six million Americans marched in New York, Chicago, San Francisco, and several other cities without bloodshed or violence of any kind. I heard some aging veterans of the sixties complain that these protests were too tame, too controlled, too lacking in passion. Maybe they were, but I wonder if the memory of what happened when passions got out of control was in the minds of some people on both sides of the barricades. Of course there was a more concrete reason for the calm. Klesta gave it to me in two words: "The draft." Thirty-five years ago, young men were not marching strictly for principle but for their lives, and young women were marching for the lives of their classmates, their brothers, lovers, and friends. At any rate, no one lost his or her life in 2003, no one ended up paralyzed for life like Dean Kahler.

If Kent State in some way affected how those protests were conducted, then the four dead, in giving their lives, however unwillingly, saved others. However, Hensley and Lewis do not limit the effects to that. In their paper, titled "The May 4 Shootings at Kent State University: The Search for Historical Accuracy," they cite comments made by top Nixon aide H. R. Haldeman in his book, *The Ends of Power*, to suggest that the shootings deepened paranoia in the White House about the antiwar movement and accelerated the slide into the conspiratorial thinking that resulted in Watergate and the eventual destruction of the Nixon administration.

On another level, the two authors continue, the massacre has come "to symbolize a great American tragedy which occurred at the height of the Vietnam era, a period in which the nation found itself deeply divided both politically and culturally. The poignant picture of Mary Vecchio kneeling in agony over Jeffrey Miller's body . . . will remain forever as a reminder of the day when the Vietnam War came home to America . . . Kent State and the Vietnam War era remain controversial even today, and the need for healing continues to exist."

A Methodist minister who played an instrumental role in the victims' attempts to obtain justice, the Rev. John Adams, describes the shootings as the bloody culmination of the Revolt of Youth in the 1960s. The Vietnam War, he says, exacerbated the conflict between generations, and it all came to a climax "on a hill and in a parking lot . . . a predictable event that took place due to the latent violence that was bound to be expressed eventually. The educated youth of the era was a natural target for this violence because of the challenges it waged against so many parts of the society confident of their rightness."

In his view, as in Klesta's, the incident at Kent opened people's eyes, compelling them to see what was happening in America. "It was symbolic," he continues, "that the military—not the police—but the military, complete with uniforms and arms, was involved because this reminded people of the war. People point to Kent State as a turning point just like the assassinations of John and Robert Kennedy and Martin Luther King. People's lives were changed in that thirteen seconds of gunfire."

Still others, among them survivor Alan Canfora, point to

a series of far-reaching events that in their opinion were a direct or indirect result of the massacre. These are:

- The nationwide student strike.

- The U.S. Congress changed the minimum voting age from twenty-one to eighteen after May 1970.

- Congress passed the War Powers Act limiting the president's authority to wage war without congressional approval.

- The U.S. invasion of Cambodia ended just six weeks after it began.

- The U.S. withdrawal from Vietnam was accelerated.

To my mind, such claims have a tenuous validity at best. The voting age was lowered chiefly because it was manifestly unjust to draft eighteen-year-olds for military service without giving them the franchise; and if men were allowed to vote at eighteen, women had to be as well. The War Powers Act arose out of Congress's recognition that it had abrogated its constitutional authority to declare war when it passed the Tonkin Gulf Resolution in 1964, giving Pres. Lyndon Johnson the green light to send troops to Vietnam. From its outset, the Cambodian invasion was planned to be of limited duration. While the incident at Kent State was the subject of much discussion in the Nixon administration, I know of no evidence that it motivated Nixon or his aides to hasten the withdrawal from Cambodia. Nor do I know of any to support the assertion that it quickened the pullout of American troops from Vietnam; the process of "Vietnamization" was well under way before the shootings. In any case, it would be two full years before the last American combat troops were brought home, which hardly suggests a sense of heightened urgency in the White House or the Pentagon. Kent State's biggest impact was to ignite the nationwide campus strike; although the strike was the first of its kind and demonstrated how widespread disaffection was in American universities, Washington did not change its policies because of it.

I also have to disagree with Klesta and Adams on one of their points—and please keep in mind that mine are not the opinions of a scholar or historian but merely those of a journalist who happened to be there when the students were shot and for a few days afterward. I fondly wish May 4 had changed hearts in the nation, compelling citizens to see the horrors the state was perpetrating in their name. But I recall the comments heard with my own ears after the killing— "should have shot more of them . . . got what they deserved . . ." and the brutal letters written to Florence Schroeder, the outcomes of the civil and criminal trials, the polls that showed the vast majority of Americans supported the guardsmen, and I conclude that the only change it had wrought in hearts was to harden them.

Hensley's and Lewis's assertion that the era remains controversial is certainly true. That was dramatically illustrated during the 2004 presidential race, when debates over Sen. John Kerry's and Pres. George Bush's war records bumped other issues off the agenda. Democratic partisans criticized Bush's service in the Texas Air National Guard, and groups backing the president, like the Swift Boat Veterans for Truth, spent millions to discredit Kerry's heroic record as a Navy patrol boat commander. With American troops fighting new wars in Iraq and Afghanistan, with the country hemorrhaging jobs overseas, and forty-six million Americans without health care, younger voters were baffled. It sounded as if Vietnam were still a hot issue. Strangely, it was, for those cultural and political rifts Hensley and Lewis mentioned were (and are) still with us, having taken new form in the division of the country into "red" and "blue" states.

Nor did the controversy over Kent State end with the 1979 settlement of the civil law suit. Over the protests of survivors and the victims' families, a gym annex was built on part of the massacre site, bringing charges that the university was trying to ignore what had happened there.

In 1980, a George Segal sculpture themed on the Old Testament story of Abraham and Isaac was offered to memorialize the incident, but was rejected as too controversial by the KSU administration and taken to Princeton University, where it stands today. In 1984, after the university agreed to build a monument, a national design competition produced hundreds of proposals. The first-place entry was rejected when the designer refused to bow to university officials' demands for control of the project. The second-place design, which would have cost over a million dollars, was scrapped when the American Legion and various conservative groups complained the memorial would be "a memorial to terrorists." It wasn't until 1990 that the current memorial was installed, and it was not dedicated to the victims but to "the events of May 4."

Alan Canfora came in for sharp criticism, some of it from people otherwise sympathetic to the victims. Writer William Gordon questioned if Canfora's actions during the protests helped to get his fellow students killed and wounded, and alleged that Canfora lied to the FBI and to a civil jury about his involvement in the demonstrations that preceded the shootings. According to Gordon, Canfora portrayed himself as an innocent bystander. Only later, he states, did Canfora proudly advertise his radical credentials and admit that he was "in the thick of things." Ever the activist, he formed the Kent May 4 Center (a nonprofit organization not affiliated with the university's May Fourth Resource Center) with his sister and several friends in 1989 to, in his words, "educate about the murder cover-up and try to prevent another Kent

State–style massacre." His zealous efforts caused some people to question his motives. In a 1991 article in the *New Republic* he was compared to a cult leader, and painted as a self-serving publicity hound who had made a career of a tragedy.

So if the degree of controversy it creates were the sole criterion for judging whether an event is a "turning point," then the Kent State Massacre would be equal to the Boston Massacre. I don't think it is. Depictions of Kent State as a pivotal moment in American history strike me as well-intentioned attempts to redeem it from falling into the maw of meaninglessness by overstating its significance. This is not to imply that I think it had no meaning or that Allison Krause, Jeff Miller, Sandy Scheuer, and William Schroeder died for no reason.

My own argument is, if you will, existential. The "events of May 4" have no meaning apart from the one we give to them, and it is incumbent, now that we are fighting another morally dubious war, to do so. The Kent State Massacre's major anniversaries have been marked with candlelit processions, with speeches and eulogies. It has been the subject of a number of symposiums and documentaries, which are all to the good. If we ignore and forget it, if we fail to draw lessons from it, then, yes, it will be pointless and the deaths suffered there mean no more than if they had been suffered in a highway collision.

And what are those lessons?

- That even in a democracy like ours, the state, if it is not led by wise and temperate people and if it perceives itself to be executing the popular will, will resort to deadly force to silence those who disagree with its policies too loudly or too vigorously.

- Because government in a representative democracy is the means the people choose to exercise their will, the people must be careful whom they elect and still more careful about communicating what they wish their representatives to do. Assuming we agree with a particular policy, we must tolerate opposing points of view and avoid branding those who dissent, even when their methods or speech offend us, as unpatriotic subversives who deserve to be imprisoned, injured, or even killed. I don't know what was going on in the minds of those guardsmen when they pulled the triggers, but I'm convinced they would not have fired it if they hadn't thought they had a license to do it and if they didn't believe they would not be punished for it. Governor Rhodes and Brigadier General Canterbury, among others, gave them the license and helped them get away with it; but the governor and the general and other leaders were acting as agents of the people's will. The people, some actively, some passively, *wanted* to teach dissenters a harsh lesson—the polls after May 4 showed this—and if the lesson involved "a bloodbath," in then Governor Reagan's felicitous phrase, so be it. In that sense, everyone was guilty.

- That a citizen who believes his or her government to be in the wrong has the right to protest through peaceful civil disobedience, when all other means to redress the wrong have been exhausted.

"Must the citizen ever for a moment, or in the least degree, resign his conscience to the legislator?" asks Thoreau in his essay *Civil Disobedience*. "Why has every man a conscience, then? . . . It is not desirable to cultivate a respect for law, so much as for the right. The only obligation which I have a right to assume is to do at any time what I think right."

Jeffrey Miller had told his mother that he didn't think the rally would accomplish much, but that he should participate and take a stand for what he thought was right. The rally had been banned (though only because guard and university officials had mistaken Governor Rhodes's words as a declaration of martial law). Miller followed his conscience rather than the law, and for that he was shot through the head.

I stress that civil disobedience must be peaceful (Thoreau, for example, expressed his objections to slavery and the Mexican War by refusing to pay his taxes) because with the right comes the responsibility to use it wisely. Violence, once it begins, attains an autonomous life independent of those who perpetrate it. Assuming its own fierce logic, the act leading inevitably to the counteraction, it becomes as mindless in its destruction as a tornado, and those who fail to recognize this truth are fools, if not criminals. The antiwar protestor has no more right to bomb, shoot, or burn than does the antiabortion protestor. There is also a pragmatic reason for nonviolence. Under the leadership of Martin Luther King and his successors, who drew inspiration from Thoreau and Gandhi, the civil rights movement broke many unjust laws but with remarkable self-discipline never resorted to the gun. It thus achieved far more to secure the rights of African-Americans than the Black Panthers or the Black Liberation Army, whose major accomplishments were to get themselves and some other people killed.

By drawing these lessons from May 1970, and putting them into practice, we will save the names of Krause, Miller, Scheuer, and Schroeder from obscurity and do the most honor to their memory.

Appendix I

Timeline of Kent State Events

Chronology, May 1–4, 1970

May 1

On Friday, May 1, students organized a demonstration to protest the invasion of Cambodia. A copy of the Constitution was buried to symbolize its "murder." A second meeting was called for noon, Monday, May 4.

On Friday evening, warm weather, drinking, and indignation over the invasion of Cambodia resulted in a crowd that moved toward the center of town breaking some windows. Police met and dispersed the crowd at the intersection of Main and Water streets. The Kent city mayor viewed the scene, heard rumors of a radical plot, declared a state of emergency, and telephoned the governor in Columbus for assistance. A National Guard officer was immediately dispatched. Bars were closed by local authorities and hundreds of people were forced into the streets and herded toward the campus with tear gas from riot-geared police. The town was quiet by 2:30 a.m.

May 2

On Saturday, students assisted with the downtown cleanup. Rumors concerning radical activities were widespread and threats to merchants confirmed the fears of some townspeople. University officials obtained an injunction prohibiting damage to buildings on campus. Notice of this injunction appeared in leaflets distributed by the Office of Student Affairs.

Shortly after 8:00 p.m., more than one thousand persons surrounded the barracks housing the Army Reserve Officer Training Corps on campus and a few managed to set the building afire. Firemen left the scene after hoses were punctured and cut open, unable to extinguish the blaze. By midnight, the National Guard cleared the campus, forcing students and nonstudents into dormitories, where many spent the night.

Appendix I

May 3

On Sunday there was a deceptively calm city and campus, occupied by National Guardsmen. Meetings produced a number of conflicting perceptions, resulting in misunderstandings among state, local, and university officials. A deluge of sightseers added to the problems. Near dusk, a crowd gathered on the Commons at the Victory Bell (a bell ordinarily rung after athletic victories). The crowd failed to disperse. At 9:00 p.m. the Ohio Riot Act was read and tear gas was fired.

The demonstrators reassembled at the intersection of East Main and Lincoln streets, blocking traffic. They believed that officials would speak to them, but no one arrived. The crowd became hostile and at 11:00 p.m. the Riot Act was read again, tear gas was used, and a number of people—guardsmen and demonstrators—were injured in the confusion.

The confrontation of Sunday night caused antagonism and resentment among all parties. Classes resumed on Monday. Demonstrators were determined to hold the rally at noon, even if prohibited. The National Guard resolved to disperse any assembly.

May 4

By noon, May 4, two thousand people had gathered in the vicinity of the Commons. Many knew that the rally had been banned. Others, especially commuters, did not know of this prohibition. Chants, curses, and rocks answered an order to disperse. Shortly after noon, tear gas canisters were fired. The gas, blowing in the wind, had little effect. The guard moved forward with fixed bayonets, forcing demonstrators to retreat. Reaching the crest of the hill by Taylor Hall, the guard moved the demonstrators even further to a nearby athletic practice field. Once on the practice field, the guard recognized that the crowd had not dispersed and, further, that the field was fenced on three sides. Tear gas was traded for more rocks and verbal abuse.

The guardsmen then retraced their line of march. Some demonstrators followed as close as twenty yards, but most were between sixty and seventy-five yards behind the guard. Near the crest of Blanket Hill, the guard turned and twenty-eight guardsmen fired between sixty-one and sixty-seven shots in thirteen seconds toward the parking lot. Four persons lay dying and nine wounded. The closest casualty was twenty yards and the farthest was almost two hundred and fifty yards away. All thirteen were students at Kent State University. The four students who were killed were Jeffrey Miller, Allison Krause, William Schroeder, and Sandra Scheuer. The nine wounded students were Joseph Lewis, John Cleary, Thomas Grace, Alan Canfora, Dean Kahler,

Appendix I

Douglas Wrentmore, James Russell, Robert Stamps, and Donald MacKenzie. Dean Kahler was permanently paralyzed from his injury.

Disbelief, fright, and attempts at first aid gave way quickly to anger. A group of two hundred to three hundred demonstrators gathered on a slope nearby and were ordered to move. Faculty members were able to convince the group to disperse.

A University ambulance moved through the campus making the following announcement over a public address system: "By order of President White, the university is closed. Students should pack their things and leave the campus as quickly as possible." Late that afternoon, the county prosecutor obtained an injunction closing the university indefinitely. Normal campus activities did not resume until the summer session.

May 5, 1970 (Tuesday)

University employees are told to remain at home until further notice. Pres. Robert White had announced on May 4 the university was closed. Students were sent home on May 4.

At a news conference Pres. Robert White calls for a federal commission to investigate problems at Kent, "a full report with complete conclusions . . . one that will reveal evidence, witnesses and conclusions."

Ohio Gov. James A. Rhodes calls for FBI director J. Edgar Hoover to begin an investigation of the shootings.

The Pentagon states it will not investigate the shootings because National Guard troops were on nonfederal status and under the command of the state of Ohio.

Six Kent students meet with Rep. William Stanton, whose congressional district includes Kent. The students then meet with presidential assistant John D. Ehrlichman. An invitation from Pres. Richard M. Nixon follows.

May 6, 1970 (Wednesday)

Pres. Richard Nixon meets with six Kent students at the White House. The six students, who claim membership in no group, are: Tom Brubach of Mantua; Dick Cutler of Kent; Don Grant of Ridgewood, New Jersey; Dean Powell of Cuyahoga Falls; Don Tretnik of Wickliffe; and Sam Trago of Northhampton.

The National Guard troops begin a phased withdrawal from Kent. About half the contingent moves out.

Sen. Mike Mansfield of Montana, Democratic leader of the Senate, proposes an investigation by a high-level commission be initiated.

May 7, 1970 (Thursday)

The Kent State University Faculty Senate and President White authorize college deans to seek to complete instruction obligations of the quarter by the best possible means. This action would allow the Ohio Board of Regents to distribute subsidy appropriations for May and June.

The faculty Senate announces support for White.

White calls for a meeting of the entire faculty for the following day.

A court injunction issued closing the campus is modified to allow the return to campus of all regular rank full-time faculty members between 8:00 a.m. and 5:00 p.m. Monday through Friday.

In addition, the president, board of trustees, full-time staff members, and full-time civil service employees are permitted to return to campus.

May 8, 1970 (Friday)

White announces that the university will stay closed through the spring quarter, which ends June 13 (Saturday). (The president had announced on May 4 that the university was closed and students were sent home.)

White also announced that university regional campuses and the university school (for grades kindergarten through 12) will reopen Monday, May 11.

The last National Guard troops leave campus in the morning. The final Ohio State Highway Patrol officers leave later in the day.

Some one hundred FBI agents are at work conducting an investigation on campus and in the city of Kent.

May 10, 1970 (Sunday)

University trustees meet with White and reaffirm closing the university and cancellation of all university-related activities for the quarter. Arrangements are made for refunds of room-and-board payments.

Trustees second White's request for a high-level federal commission study.

May 11, 1970 (Monday)

White announces the formation of a twenty-eight-member faculty-staff-student Commission on Kent State University Violence (CKSUV) to explore completely the incidents of May 1–4 and to help prevent any recurrence of violence. The chairman is Dr. Harold M. Mayer, university professor of geography.

The commission immediately issues an "urgent request" for people with information concerning events on campus or in the city in early May to contact the group and make such information known.

"No details should be considered too insignificant to mention," Mayer said.

"What may appear unimportant to the person possessing the information might enlarge the commission's total understanding of what happened those days, and why."

It is revealed that the commission would honor the confidence of all statements received but that its (the commission's) files may be subject to subsequent subpoena by official bodies.

Robert H. Finch, then secretary of Health, Education and Welfare, meets with White while in Ohio for a speaking engagement. Finch is the first cabinet officer to visit the campus since the May 4 tragedy.

Finch adds his voice to those calling for a presidential commission to study campus violence. After the meeting with White, Finch sends the following to Washington, D.C.:

"President Richard M. Nixon: Respectfully but urgently I renew plea for high level investigating commission to delve into KSU events to clarify evidence, furnish perspective and do so in a way fully credible publicly. In this I join with Congressman Stanton and Senators Mansfield and Scott."

May 13, 1970 (Wednesday)
The court injunction is modified to allow graduate assistants, temporary instructors, and construction workers back on campus.

May 15, 1970 (Friday)
An ad hoc student government commission is formed to explore the possibility of holding the June 13 commencement as planned.

Portage County prosecutor Ron Kane holds a press conference to display weapons and materials found in a search of campus rooms after May 4. On display are a pistol, shotgun, machetes, five containers of marijuana, cap pistols, slingshots, hunting knives, BB guns, and cold pills.

Several students and professors viewing the display call it "meager" and said a like collection could probably be found by searching any one square block of the city.

Lawyers from the American Civil Liberties Union denounce the display and call the search unconstitutional.

May 18, 1970 (Monday)
Rep. J. William Stanton of Ohio meets with White and backs his request for a federal investigation.

The first contingent of generally somber students returns to campus to pick up their belongings in residence halls.

May 19, 1970 (Tuesday)
A forty-five-member commission to implement a commitment to NonViolence is established under the chairmanship of Charles E. Kegley, then assistant professor of health and physical education.

The commission has a twofold task:

(1) to consider and recommend various control procedures including, but not restricted to, a marshaling program, group discussions, and the development of an administrative policy in response to violence or threats of violence;
(2) to attempt to prevent violence by identifying those conditions that might produce it and to suggest means by which to eliminate them.

May 21, 1970 (Thursday)

Attorney General John N. Mitchell announces he is stepping up the Justice Department's investigations of the shootings to determine as soon as possible whether there have been criminal violations of federal laws in the shootings at Kent and deaths of two black students at Jackson State University in Mississippi (May 14, 1970, Thursday).

May 24, 1970 (Sunday)

White House Director of Communications Herbert G. Klein announces the formation of a commission to investigate the Kent State tragedy.

May 28, 1970 (Thursday)

Following a modification of a court order to allow graduates to return for spring commencement, the Kent State University board of trustees votes to proceed with plans to hold commencement on June 13 as scheduled.

June 6, 1970 (Saturday)

One of the last acts of the Ohio state legislature before the summer recess was to pass a new campus riot bill, which will become law in September (1970).

The bill is designed to require swift action against students and faculty charged during disturbances at state-assisted colleges and universities.

The bill provides strict penalties for outsiders convicted of a variety of changes on campuses. The same penalties apply to students and faculty who could also be suspended from their school pending a court decision on their case.

The bill would require a hearing within five days of their arrest with an attorney appointed by the Ohio Board of Regents serving as a referee. Court conviction would mean a mandatory one-year dismissal. Reinstatement would be automatic if found innocent by the court and in this case the record of suspension would be erased.

June 9, 1970 (Tuesday)

An Ohio unit of the American Civil Liberties Union issues a report protesting the direction of the FBI inquiry. ACLU complaints center on complaints from students and faculty that FBI agents were investigating political beliefs and teachings of some professors.

June 10, 1970 (Wednesday)

Arthur Krause, father of Allison Krause, one of the four students killed, files a $6 million suit in federal court against Gov. James A. Rhodes and two Ohio National Guard commanders. His suit states the defendants "intentionally and maliciously disregarded the lives and safety of students, spectators, and passersby, including Allison Krause."

Krause also files a $2 million suit in Portage County Common Pleas Court against the state of Ohio.

June 13, 1970 (Saturday)

Forty days after their forced exodus from campus some 1,250 seniors and graduate students return en masse to receive degrees.

Early in the commencement ceremony a telephone on the speaker's platform rang quietly. Unnoticed by many in the audience, the phone was passed to President White. In the middle of his address the president digressed momentarily to say the call had been from Rep. William J. Stanton.

Word had come from the White House that President Nixon had named a special commission to investigate campus unrest.

President Nixon releases the names of those serving on a nine-member commission to examine campus violence and recommend ways of peacefully resolving student grievances and avoid future incidents such as the one at Kent. The commission's mandate has been broadened to include the Jackson State deaths and campus violence overall.

The panel is headed by former Pennsylvania Gov. William W. Scranton. Also on the panel are:

James Ahern, chief of police for New Haven, Conn.

Erwin D. Canham, editor in chief of the *Christian Science Monitor*

Dr. James E. Cheek, president of Howard University, Washington, D.C.

Benjamin O. Davis, public safety director of the city of Cleveland, Ohio

Martha A. Derthick, professor of political science at Boston College, Chestnut Hill, Mass.

Appendix I

Bayless Manning, dean of the Stanford University
Law School at Stanford, Calif.

Revius O. Ortique of New Orleans, La., lawyer and past
president of the National Bar Association, a predominantly
black organization.

Joseph Rhodes, Jr., a junior fellow at Harvard University at
Cambridge, Mass., and former student president at the
California Institute of Technology at Pasadena, Calif.

June 15, 1970 (Monday)

A court injunction that closed the campus May 4 is lifted in
order for summer classes to begin.

As a result of the order lifted by Judge Albert Caris, juris-
diction of the campus is returned to the board of trustees.

June 19, 1970 (Friday)

Summer quarter begins at Kent.

June 22, 1970 (Monday)

Summer classes begin.

The first summer session begins with an enrollment of
7,470, slightly less than the summer enrollment of 7,679 a
year ago.

Appendix I

July 23, 1970 (Thursday)

A Justice Department report on the Kent shootings is revealed in an article published in the *Akron Beacon Journal*. Details in a ten-page Justice Department memo summarize the reports of one hundred FBI agents. The article quotes Jerris Leonard, chief of the civil rights division for the Justice Department, who said that the shootings "were not necessary and not in order" and that about two hundred demonstrators heckling the guardsmen could have been repulsed by more tear gas and arrests, there was no hail of rocks thrown before the shooting, that no guardsmen were hit by rocks or other projectiles and no guardsmen were in danger of losing their lives.

The statements in the memo and report differ greatly from accounts provided previously by Ohio officials and guard officers.

The department also states that FBI investigators determined that the shooting lasted eleven seconds and altogether thirteen people were hit—four in the front and nine in the side or back.

A Justice Department statement confirms the memo included options for prosecution. The statement reads: "If Mr. (Ronald) Kane chooses to release such information, he must bear responsibility for it."

Kane responds that the FBI report would be used in a grand jury investigation. "Nothing has been released about this from this office and nothing can until it is given to the grand jury," Kane states.

July 24, 1970 (Friday)

Maj. Gen. Sylvester T. Del Corso, adjutant general of the Ohio National Guard, states the FBI assertions "are not factual . . . They fail to include many facts which we provided."

"The conclusions as stated in the paper by the reporter are just unbelievable . . . that there were no troops injured, that no stones were thrown, and that there was a question whether there even was a riot," Del Corso said.

August 1, 1970 (Saturday)

Del Corso, Ohio guard commander, urges a grand jury be convened. Del Corso's request comes following reports of a Justice Department memo indicating that National Guardsmen could be held liable to criminal charges in the shootings.

August 3, 1970 (Monday)

Rhodes orders state Attorney General Paul W. Brown to convene a special Portage County grand jury to investigate the shootings. Portage County prosecutor Ron Kane said previously that the county did not have the money needed to conduct an investigation. Rhodes's action enables investigation costs to be handled by the state.

August 7, 1970 (Friday)

J. Edgar Hoover sends a letter to John S. Knight, president and editor of the *Akron Beacon Journal*. Hoover charges the paper with distorting the facts in the July 23, 1970, article about the FBI investigation. In his letter, Hoover denies that the FBI concluded that the shootings were unnecessary as reported in the paper. Hoover adds that the results of the FBI inquiry were turned over to the Justice Department "without recommendation or conclusion."

August 19–21, 1970 (Wednesday–Friday)

The President's Commission on Campus Unrest convenes in Kent. The public hearings are the final series by the panel before submitting its report.

Among those testifying are Dr. Robert I. White, president of Kent State University; Maj. Gen. Sylvester T. Del Corso, Ohio National Guard adjutant general; Brig. Gen. Robert H. Canterbury, who commanded the troops at Kent; James C. Woodring, Jr., student witness; and George Warren, staff investigator for the commission.

Warren testifies that the FBI has "concluded that no other person than a guardsman fired a weapon." Ballistics reports indicated that twenty-nine guardsmen fired at least fifty-four shots during the rifle volley that resulted in the deaths of four and wounding of nine others.

White testifies August 19. His testimony differs from Canterbury's testimony (to be given the next day) as to whether the university requested the troops on campus and whether White specifically asked guard officials to prevent a student rally May 4.

White said that "by and large the National Guard was in charge." Canterbury, however, contends that the guard was acting in response to university requests.

Kent Mayor Leroy Satrom testifies August 20 and Kent police chief Roy Thompson testifies on August 21. They both contend that disturbances were planned and initiated by outside militants. White's testimony of August 19 indicates that Kent had been "targeted" for disruptions by radicals "interested in either doing some burning or shutting us down."

September 15, 1970 (Tuesday)
A special state grand jury of fifteen members is sworn in in Ravenna, which is the county seat of Portage County where Kent and Kent State are located.

Appendix I

September 26, 1970 (Saturday)

The President's Commission on Campus Unrest makes public its general report on the Kent shootings. The report describes the National Guard shootings as "unwarranted." The panel adds, however, that "violent and criminal" actions by students contributed to the tragedy.

The panel emphasizes that the tragedy was not unique, stating, "Only the magnitude of the student disorder and the extent of student deaths and injuries set it apart from the occurrences on numerous other American campuses during the past few years."

The panel says "indiscriminate firing" by guardsmen was "unnecessary, unwarranted, and inexcusable." The commission adds, "Those who wreaked havoc on the town of Kent, those who burned the ROTC building, those who attacked and stoned National Guardsmen and all those who urged them on share the responsibility for the deaths and injuries of May 4."

The report goes on to state, "no one would have died" if the guard had followed recommendations by the National Advisory Commission on Civil Disorder and U.S. Army guidelines, both of which advise against "general issuance of loaded weapons to law enforcement officers engaged in controlling disorders" that fall short of "armed resistance."

The report's most important conclusion is, "The Kent State tragedy must surely mark the last time that loaded rifles are issued as a matter of course to guardsmen confronting student demonstrators."

A great deal of the report provides a detailed chronology of the four days of events leading to the shootings. The report paints a picture of weary and frightened guardsmen and students unsure of the permissible limits of dissent and hostile actions over the presence of troops on campus.

October 16, 1970 (Friday)

Convening in Ravenna, a special state grand jury indicts twenty-five people on charges stemming from the disturbances at Kent. No guardsmen are indicted.

The jury finds that the guardsmen were not "subject to criminal prosecution" because they "fired their weapons in the honest and sincere belief . . . that they would suffer serious bodily injury had they not done so." The jury adds that weapons used by the guardsmen were "not appropriate in quelling campus disorders," but the jury's exoneration of guard action contrasts with the President's Commission on Campus Unrest, which stated October 4, 1970, that the shootings were "unnecessary, unwarranted, and inexcusable."

In the eighteen-page report, the jury sets the "major responsibility" for the disturbances as resting "clearly with those persons who are charged with the administration of the University." According to the panel, the administration "over a period of several years" had "fostered an attitude of laxity, overindulgence, and permissiveness with its students and faculty to the extent that it can no longer regulate the activities of either." What the jury describes as the university's "overemphasis . . . on the right to dissent" is also severely criticized.

Attorney General John Mitchell states that the Justice Department is continuing to investigate the shootings and will review the state grand jury findings.

October 19–26, 1970 (Monday–Monday)

Names of defendants charged by a special state grand jury are released as arrests begin. Among those charged are Craig Morgan, twenty-one, Kent student body president, with second-degree riot, and Dr. Thomas S. Lough, sociology professor, with inciting to riot. Both are released on bail.

By October 26, one nonstudent and fifteen current or former students are charged with various crimes including riot, assault, and arson. Many are as a result of the burning of the ROTC building on May 2, 1970.

October 20, 1970 (Tuesday)

The Kent State University Faculty Senate, the Student Senate, and the Graduate Student Council issue a joint statement demanding a federal grand jury investigation.

William Kuntsler, attorney for the Chicago Seven, arrives in Kent to help coordinate the defense of the twenty-five people charged.

1971

January 28, 1971 (Thursday)

U.S. District Court Judge William K. Thomas, ruling in Cleveland, upholds the twenty-five grand jury indictments. Thomas also rules that the report issued by the jury is illegal and orders it be destroyed in ten days.

In his ruling, Thomas states that the report, if allowed to stand, would "irreparably injure" the defendants' rights to a fair trial. He adds that the jury "violated the oath of secrecy . . . took over the duties of a petit (regular) jury and acted as a trying body and determined guilt" and issued a report that is illegal in that it "advises, condemns, or commends."

Thomas also rules on two suits brought by faculty members and students (including ten under indictment). His ruling lets stand the indictments because "bad faith in the sense of deliberate willful pervision of law to gain an improper purpose is not directly shown and it will not be inferred."

Thomas adds that decisions on whether the twenty-five could have fair trials could be made when jury selection begins in each trial. According to Thomas, then former Gov. James A. Rhodes was in error in calling for a grand jury report. "Governor Rhodes's call appears to direct the special grand jury to identify causes," Thomas said.

The jury report "renders moral and social judgments on policies, attitudes, and conduct of the university administration and some faculty and students," according to Thomas.

Further, the jury accused the administration of "permissiveness" with its faculty and students and also criticized faculty members of "overemphasis in dissent." These were violations of rights of free expression of people not under indictment, according to Thomas.

Thomas criticizes the jury for claiming witnesses "have fairly represented every aspect, attitude, and point of view concerning the events." Instead, the findings should have been based on "probable cause." Thomas's criticism specifically points to the finding that the events constituted a riot. He argues that this finding should be left to a regular grand jury and that "establishing existence of a riot is a basic and essential element of at least twenty-seven of forty-three charged offences" in the indictments.

Thomas also states that the jury's finding that National Guardsmen, who killed four students at Kent, acted in self-defense "is another ways of saying that the 'rioters' are guilty."

February 18, 1971 (Thursday)
President White submits his resignation, effective September 15, 1971.

May 5, 1971 (Wednesday)
Demonstrators end an overnight sit-in in front of the Reserve Officers Training Corps headquarters in protest of ROTC on campus (then located in Rockwell Hall).

May 14, 1971 (Friday)
A probe of the Jackson State University and Kent State University killings is called when a group of national religious leaders urge that federal grand jury investigations begin. The leaders claim that Mississippi and Ohio state grand ju-

ries had exonerated law enforcement officers without examining all the evidence.

The statement reads, "In a nation that genuinely respects law and order, policemen are not above the law nor students below it . . . We call upon the U.S. Department of Justice to rectify this situation by prosecuting those responsible."

The statement is distributed at a memorial service for the slain students held at a Washington, D.C., church. Among those attending are Mr. and Mrs. Arthur Krause, parents of Allison, one of the four killed at Kent, and Dale Gibbs, widow of Phillip Gibbs, one of two killed at Jackson State on May 14, 1970.

The statement was signed by:

Dr. Cynthia Wedel, president of the
National Council of Churches

Rabbi Maurice N. Eisendrath, president of the
Union of American Hebrew Congregations

United Methodist Bishop Charles F. Golden

Mrs. Wayne W. Harrington of the
United Methodist Board of Missions

Rabbi Solomon J. Sharman, president of the
Synagogue Council of America

Appendix I

Rev. A. Dudley Ward, general secretary of the United Methodist Board of Christian Social Concerns

Rev. Geno Baroni, director of the National Center for Urban Ethnic Affairs

May 24, 1971 (Monday)

A group of twenty U.S. congressmen request a Justice Department investigation.

July 22, 1971 (Thursday)

Peter Davies's report is published. The private report is funded by the Department of Law, Justice and Community Relations of the United Methodist Church's Board of Christian Social Concerns. Davies writes that a small group of guardsmen had agreed to "punish" the students and opened fire on signal.

The 227-page analysis is based on testimony already on public record. Davies cites a "monumental accumulation of testimony and photographs which support the theory that the shooting was planned and carried out with the intent to kill, maim, or injure students."

The report had been submitted to the Justice Department for a month previous. When the department makes no response to the report's "appeal" for an "immediate and thorough" federal investigation, the report is released.

Davies states that "a few guardsmen, perhaps no more than eight to ten," from G Troop of the 107th Armored Cavalry had decided to shoot at students "at an opportune moment." Davies said most of the guardsmen involved in the shooting "did indeed fire in reaction to those who triggered the shooting by their willful firing."

July 23, 1971 (Friday)

A $4 million lawsuit against the state of Ohio filed by Louis Schroeder in connection with the death of his son William is dismissed by U.S. District Court Judge James C. Connell in Cleveland.

As in three previous suits filed by the parents of the dead students, his ruling is the same: the state has sovereign immunity and cannot be sued unless it consents.

(See also June 10, 1970)

August 2, 1971 (Monday)

Glenn Olds is named president of Kent State University by the board of trustees.

Appendix I

August 6, 1971 (Friday)

U.S. Congress begins recess.

August 13, 1971 (Friday)

Attorney General John N. Mitchell announces that no federal grand jury will be empaneled to investigate the shootings at Kent. "There is no credible evidence of a conspiracy between National Guardsmen to shoot students on campus," Mitchell said.

He also said Justice Department investigations supported the conclusion of the President's Commission on Campus Unrest that the guardsmen's rifle fire was "unnecessary, unwarranted and inexcusable." But no conspiracy had been discovered and a grand jury could not be expected to produce new evidence beyond that already provided by the commission and FBI, Mitchell said.

"There is no likelihood of successful prosecutions of individual guardsmen," he said.

Rep. William Moorhead of Pennsylvania, who was one of the twenty congressmen requesting a probe on May 24, releases a statement: "We predicted this response by the attorney general and we're not surprised by it."

Moorehead had communicated to other signers of the request that the Justice Department announcement regarding the decision not to pursue the case would be made "sometime during Congressional recess . . . to minimize Congressional response." Congress recessed August 6.

August 14, 1971 (Saturday)

James F. Ahern, a member of the president's commission, responds to Mitchell's announcement that it is "incredible" that the attorney general failed to order a grand jury investigation and that the decision was "inconceivable . . . in the face of the FBI report indicating there was probable cause to file criminal charges."

September 13, 1971 (Monday)

Martin C. Pryor, an Ohio National Guard sergeant, files a $1.5 million libel suit against Peter Davies in connection with statements in the Davies report released July 22, 1971.

September 15, 1971 (Wednesday)

President White's resignation is effective. Glenn Olds takes over officially as president.

September 29, 1971 (Wednesday)

A U.S. District Court judge rules that the Ohio National Guard must discharge Raymond D. Silvey, who had declared himself a conscientious objector after being present at Kent during the shootings.

September 30, 1971 (Thursday)

The Ohio Eighth District Court of Appeals orders a lower court to consider on its merits the suit against Ohio's claim to immunity from civil suits resulting from actions of state agents.

October 20, 1971 (Wednesday)

A petition signed by 10,380 Kent students and faculty members is presented to Pres. Richard Nixon requesting a federal probe of the killings. The petition is referred to Attorney General John Mitchell.

October 22, 1971 (Friday)

A U.S. Circuit Court of Appeals upholds a 1970 order by Portage County Common Pleas Court Judge Edwin W. Jones that prohibits discussion of the May 4 incident and case by three hundred witnesses and others connected with the grand jury and indictments.

Appendix I

November 15, 1971 (Monday)

The Portage County grand jury report is officially burned as ordered by the Sixth Circuit U.S. Court of Appeals, which upheld a lower court ruling of October 26 also ordering the report destroyed as prejudicial.

The court upholds the grand jury's twenty-five indictments ruling that the defense lawyers failed to establish the prosecutor's bad faith or that the defendants would "suffer great and immediate injury from prosecution."

November 19, 1971 (Friday)

The U.S. Supreme Court refuses to delay trials in Ravenna set to begin November 22. The court votes 6–1 and gives no reason for its action. Justice William O. Douglas casts the dissenting vote and writes that Ohio's antiriot laws "on their face seem overly broad" and infringe on First Amendment rights of those required to defend themselves against the charges.

November 22, 1971 (Monday)

Jury selection begins in Portage County Common Pleas Court for the trial of Jerry Rupe, the first of twenty-three students, former students, and faculty members on trial for disorders preceding the shootings.

Rupe is charged with rioting, arson, slashing a fire hose, and throwing rocks at firefighters on May 2, 1970, when the ROTC building was set afire. He was jailed in September 1971 after a $25,000 bond was withdrawn.

As the trial starts, Portage County Common Pleas Court Judge Edwin W. Jones imposes elaborate restrictions on press coverage and demonstrations. Jones prohibits attorneys, witnesses, jurors, and county employees from giving interviews to the press. Under Jones's order, picketing, parading, and passing leaflets are prohibited. Cameras and electronic equipment are off-limits in the courthouse.

An affidavit is filed on behalf of ten defendants charging Jones with "bias and prejudice" as evidenced by his convening the original grand jury and disseminating its controversial report.

November 30, 1971 (Tuesday)

Jerry Rupe is convicted in Portage County Common Pleas Court of the misdemeanor of interfering with a fireman. The jury was unable to reach a verdict on three felony charges of rioting, arson, and throwing rocks at firemen.

The state dismisses the charges against the second defendant, Peter Bliek.

Appendix I

December 1, 1971 (Wednesday)
Larry Shub pleads guilty to first-degree riot charges in Portage County Common Pleas Court. Additional charges are dropped.

December 6, 1971 (Monday)
Thomas F. Fogelsong pleads guilty to first-degree riot charges in Portage County Common Pleas Court.

December 7, 1971 (Tuesday)
Portage County Common Pleas Court Judge Edwin Jones instructs the jury to find the fifth defendant, Helen Nicholas, not guilty of interfering with a fireman. Special state prosecutor John Hayward moves to drop the remaining cases.

The state of Ohio drops all charges against twenty remaining defendants in the Portage County Common Pleas Court on grounds of lack of evidence after two of the first five defendants were cleared, two pleaded guilty, and charges against another were dismissed.

The dismissals were "not intended to vindicate nor criticize the special grand jury, the students" or any other involved party, according to Ohio Attorney General William Brown. He concluded some time before that many of the cases could not be prosecuted and had arranged the trials in order of the strongest evidence, Brown said.

1972

January 21, 1972 (Friday)
Jerry Rupe, found guilty of interfering with a fireman (misdemeanor) on May 2, 1970, is sentenced to six months in jail by Portage County Common Pleas Court Judge Edwin W. Jones. His sentence runs concurrently with an unrelated 10- to 20-year drug sentence imposed in 1971.

May 4, 1972 (Thursday)
The American Civil Liberties Union files damage suits totaling $12.1 million in Cleveland against Ohio and the Ohio National Guard in connection with the 1970 shootings at Kent.

1973

August 3, 1973 (Friday)
The Justice Department announces it will reopen the May 4, 1970, case. The announcement is made almost two years af-

ter the department rejected further federal inquiries into the case.

In his written statement, Attorney General Elliot Richardson does not mention new evidence but states that the decision to start a new inquiry rests on "the need to exhaust every potential for acquiring facts relating to this tragedy."

Assistant Attorney General J. Stanley Pottinger, head of the Civil Rights Division, will conduct the investigation.

Pottinger said he could "not speculate on any new evidence we may or may not have" but suggested that the decision had been prompted by other events, including civil suits filed by parents of victims, congressional inquiries, student petitions, and pressure for reform of National Guard procedures.

Sen. Birch Bayh of Indiana reveals he had informed Richardson of a letter sent to Bayh by a National Guard company commander suggesting that a police informer, Terrence B. Norman, might have precipitated the National Guard fire by firing his own revolver at students.

According to Bayh, the commander said Norman was posing as a newsman and had run up to guardsmen after the shootings, handed over a revolver, and said he had shot a student.

Bayh also said that FBI director Clarence M. Kelley told him on July 9 that Norman had once been an FBI informer in an unrelated matter but had not been questioned on the Kent case. A Justice Department spokesman said August 3 that the FBI had interviewed Norman twice about the May 4 incident.

December 4, 1973 (Tuesday)

Attorneys for parents of three slain students ask the Supreme Court to allow the parents to sue former Ohio Gov. James Rhodes and National Guardsmen as individuals after suits against the state and guard had been dismissed under the doctrine of sovereign immunity.

December 12, 1973 (Wednesday)

Sen. William Saxbe of Ohio tells the Senate Judiciary Committee that he would excuse himself from the Justice Department's reopened inquiry into the 1970 shootings.

December 17, 1973 (Monday)

The Senate votes 75–10 to confirm Sen. William Saxbe of Ohio as attorney general.

December 18, 1973 (Tuesday)

A federal grand jury meeting in Cleveland begins hearing evidence in the Justice Department's reopened investigation.

1974

March 29, 1974 (Friday)

A federal grand jury indicts eight former guardsmen. They are technically charged with violating the civil rights of the students. The indictment states all eight guardsmen fired in the direction of demonstrators.

Five are accused of firing the shots—from M-1 rifles—that resulted in the deaths.

The five are: James D. McGee, William E. Perkins, James E. Pierce, Lawrence A. Shafer, and Ralph W. Zoller. They face possible terms of life imprisonment.

The other three, Matthew J. McManus, Barry W. Morris, and Leon H. Smith, are charged with firing of pistols and shotguns that resulted in the injuries. They face possible maximum penalties of one year in prison and a $1,000 fine.

McManus is listed as a present guard member in the indictment. He told reporters he had resigned before the grand jury appearance.

Assistant Attorney General J. Stanley Pottinger, head of the Civil Rights Division conducting the investigation, states that the grand jury has not been discharged and could be re-convened to hear other evidence.

April 4, 1974 (Thursday)

All eight former guardsmen, indicted by a federal grand jury of charges of violating civil rights of students, plead not guilty.

An attorney for four of the defendants argues for dismissal of the charges and files motions charging the government with "gross misconduct" amounting to fraud and obstruction of justice in delaying the calling of the grand jury.

The motion argues that the defendants had "every right" to believe the case was closed when John Mitchell, then attorney general, stopped the federal investigation in 1971.

An additional motion calls for Mitchell and former Attorney General Richard Kleindienst to be made available for depositions.

April 17, 1974 (Wednesday)

The Supreme Court rules that parents of three students allegedly killed by National Guardsmen at Kent can sue Ohio officials and officers of the guard. The 8–0 decision of *Scheuer v. Rhodes* reverses a lower court decision holding state officials immune from such suits. The decision does not deal with the merits of the suit. Justice William O. Douglas does not join the ruling.

Chief Justice Warren E. Burger writes for the court, stating the established constitutional prohibition against suing a state provides "no shield for a state official confronted by the claim that he had deprived another of a federal right under the color of the law."

In this case, parents were not suing the state "but seeking to impose individual and personal liability on the named defendants" for violations of federal civil rights laws that resulted in the students' deaths, according to Burger.

He added that state officials enjoyed only qualified immunity "dependent upon the score of discretion and responsibilities of the office and all circumstances as they reasonably appeared at the time."

Federal civil rights guarantees "would be drained of meaning were we to hold that the acts of a governor or other high executive officer has the quality of supreme and unchangeable edict, overriding all conflicting rights . . . and were unreviewable by the federal courts," Burger concluded.

Appendix I

October 21, 1974 (Monday)

The federal trial of eight former National Guardsmen accused of violating civil rights of the four slain students opens in Cleveland before U.S. District Court Judge Frank J. Battisti.

The Justice Department will present thirty-three witnesses and 130 exhibits—mostly photographs of the confrontation between guardsmen and students. The twelve-member jury will visit the Kent campus, where it will hear simulated gunshots at the scene.

November 8, 1974 (Friday)

U.S. District Court Judge Frank J. Battisti acquits eight former guardsmen in Cleveland.

Battisti rules that U.S. prosecutors failed to prove charges that guardsmen willfully intended to deprive the four students killed and nine wounded of their civil rights.

"At best, the evidence . . . would support a finding that the amount of force against defendants was excessive and unjustified," Battisti said.

Battisti's opinion also cautions, "It is vital that state and National Guard officials not regard this decision as authorizing

or approving the use of force against demonstrators, whatever the occasion or the issue involved."

Assistant Attorney General J. Stanley Pottinger states that
the court ruling ended the federal government's prosecution
in the case. "The decision to reopen the case was right. The
grand jury's decision to indict was right. The trial of the case
was thorough. The department has done everything in its
power to air the causes of this tragedy and enforce the law,"
he said.

1975

May–August 1975

Civil trials begin in Cleveland before a federal jury in which
the wounded students and parents of the dead students had
filed civil suits seeking a total of $46 million in damages
from Rhodes, former Kent president Robert I. White, and
twenty-seven former and current guardsmen.

All individual suits are consolidated into one case, *Krause v.
Rhodes*. Chief attorney for the plaintiffs is Joseph Kelner of
New York.

U.S. District Court Judge Don J. Young presides.

Appendix I

During the course of the fifteen-week trial, the six-man, six-woman civil jury will hear testimony from more than one hundred witnesses. At the trial's outset, both sides agree a three-fourths majority (nine votes) is sufficient for a verdict.

Attorneys for the victims argue that the shootings were willful, indiscriminate, and in violation of the students' rights to assemble on the campus and protest the invasion of Cambodia.

Defense lawyers in turn counter that the guardsmen had been called out by civil authorities to protect life and property. The guardsmen's actions were justified because students charged the ranks, putting guardsmen in fear of their lives, according to the defense.

The defense calls witnesses who claimed to have heard nonmilitary gunfire before the guardsmen fired, as well as a former student who testified that she saw a civilian fire a gun shortly before the guardsmen began shooting.

However, Brig. Gen. Robert H. Canterbury, commander of the guardsmen and a defendant in the suits, admits in testimony that officials were unable to substantiate reports of firing by snipers, and three former students disputed their fellow student's claim that she saw a civilian fire a gun.

Appendix I

August 22, 1975 (Friday)

U.S. District Court Judge Don J. Young instructs jurors on the statutes and constitutional issues of the case. A preponderance of the evidence had to show that the defendants had violated statutory and constitutional rights of the plaintiffs, including the rights to assemble peacefully; the right not to be deprived of life and liberty without due process of the law; the right not to suffer cruel and inhuman punishment; and the right to protection against excessive government force, according to Young's instructions.

Additionally, Young instructs the jury to decide if state laws on assault and battery and negligence had been violated.

August 27, 1975 (Wednesday)

A federal court jury meeting in Cleveland exonerates Ohio Gov. James Rhodes and twenty-eight other defendants from any financial or personal responsibility in connection with the shootings. After deliberating for thirty-three hours, the vote to acquit is 9–3.

The jury's decision found that the plaintiffs had not been denied their civil rights, nor had they been victims of the "willful or wanton misconduct or of the negligence of some or all of the defendants."

1976

November 12, 1976 (Friday)

Glenn Olds, president of Kent State University, announces his resignation, which will be effective July 15, 1977.

1977

June, 1977

An appeal of the federal court jury on the civil cases is underway. Attorney Sanford Rosen of San Francisco is chosen to head the new legal team.

Oral arguments for the appeal are heard in Cincinnati at the same time the "Move the Gym" controversy is in progress. The controversy centers on whether an annex to Memorial Gym will infringe on or encroach a portion of the site where the confrontation between the guard, demonstrators, and wounded students took place.

June 9, 1977 (Thursday)

Dr. Brage Golding is elected president of Kent State University by the board of trustees.

Appendix I

July 15, 1977 (Friday)

Dr. Michael Schwartz, then vice president for academic and student affairs, begins his term as interim president. Glenn Olds's resignation is effective.

August 10, 1977 (Wednesday)

Dr. Brage Golding, newly elected president of Kent State University, arrives on the Kent campus.

September 12, 1977 (Monday)

In a reversal of the 1975 lower court ruling that had cleared those defendants charged in a damage suit resulting from the shootings, the U.S. Court of Appeals for the Sixth Circuit Court orders a retrial. The ruling states that Rhodes, several state officials, and National Guardsmen should stand trial again because at least one jury member had been "threatened and assaulted by a person interested in its outcome." A new trial for the federal civil cases is ordered, based on the judgment of the first judge, Donald Young, who had improperly made a threat against one of the jurors.

The damage suit for $46 million had been filed by those wounded and relatives of those killed during the shootings. They claim construction of the gymnasium annex would destroy physical evidence that might be relevant to the new trial.

1978

December 1978

A new trial is scheduled to begin. Young has withdrawn from the case and is replaced by William Thomas, whom plaintiffs see as more objective in his conduct of the trial.

1979

January 4, 1979 (Thursday)

An out-of-court settlement is reached in the civil cases and approved by the State Controlling Board with a vote of 6–1. The board is required to approve all state expenditures.

Shortly after the board announces its decision, the judge in the U.S. District Court in Cleveland dismisses a jury that had been called to hear testimony in a second trial against the state.

The plaintiffs receive $675,000 for injuries received in 1970 and this compensation is accompanied by a statement from the defendants, which reads in part, "In retrospect the tragedy of May 4, 1970, should not have occurred. . . . We deeply regret those events and are profoundly saddened by the deaths of four students and the wounding of nine others which resulted."

The settlement, according to the plaintiffs, "accomplished to the greatest extent possible under present law" their main objectives, not the least of which was financial support for Dean Kahler, who has been paralyzed.

Also sought by plaintiffs was a statement signed by Rhodes and twenty-seven National Guardsmen who were defendants in the case.

The statement, read in court, said: "In retrospect, the tragedy of May 4, 1970, should not have occurred."

It also noted that students protesting the Cambodian invasion by U.S. troops "may have believed they were right" in continuing their protests in spite of a university ban on rallies and an order for the students to disperse. The statement went on to note that those orders had been upheld as "lawful" by the Sixth U.S. Circuit Court of Appeals.

The statement continues:

"Some of the guardsmen on Blanket Hill (the campus area where the violence occurred), fearful and anxious from prior events, may have believed in their own minds that their lives were in danger. Hindsight suggests another method would have resolved the confrontation. Better ways must be found to deal with such confrontations.

"We devoutly wish that a means had been found to avoid the May 4 events culminating in the Guard shootings and the irreversible deaths and injuries. We deeply regret those events, and are profoundly saddened by the deaths of four students and wounding of nine others which resulted. We hope that the agreement to end this litigation will help assuage the tragic moments regarding that sad day."

Settlement of monies were distributed as follows:

Dean Kahler, $350,000
Joseph Lewis, $42,500
Thomas Grace, $37,500
Donald MacKenzie, $27,500
John Cleary, $22,500
Alan Canfora, Douglas Wrentmore, Robert Stamps,
James Russell, $15,000 each
Families of the four students slain, $15,000 each
Attorneys fees and expenses, $75,000

Appendix II

The Report of
The President's Commission
on Campus Unrest

September 1970

Preface

The President established this Commission on June 13, 1970, in the wake of the great tragedies at Kent State University in Ohio and Jackson State College in Mississippi.

The Commission held its first meeting on June 25, 1970. During the next three months it conducted thirteen days of public hearings in Washington, D.C.; Los Angeles, California; Jackson, Mississippi; and Kent, Ohio; and met fifteen times in executive session.

The Commission staff conducted intensive investigations

in Jackson; Kent; and Lawrence, Kansas, and visited for shorter periods many other colleges and universities throughout the country. These staff teams interviewed students, faculty members, and administrators. The Commission examined the available material on the subject of its mandate and commissioned a number of scholarly papers. The Commission also benefited from a number of consultants.

This report is the result of all these efforts.

One of the major barriers to rational discussion of the subject of campus unrest is that the term means many things to many people. Indeed, the term has become so general that it now embraces not only the intellectual ferment which should exist in the university but also all forms of protest, both peaceful and otherwise. The use of the term "campus unrest" in its present undifferentiated meaning is unfortunate because it blurs the distinction between the desirable and the abhorrent, between activities which the university and society should encourage or must tolerate, and those which they must seek to prevent and must deal with firmly.

As a result of the muddling of the term "unrest," the university and law enforcement agencies find themselves under pressures to stifle even peaceful and legitimate forms of unrest and to condone its violent and illegitimate forms. Pressures of this sort can only lead to confusion and injustice.

Throughout this report we stress that campus unrest is in fact a complex phenomenon that is manifested in many kinds of protest activity. Most protests, even today, are entirely peaceful and orderly manifestations of dissent, such as holding meetings, picketing, vigils, demonstrations, and marches—all of which are protected by the First Amendment.

Other protest is disorderly, that is, disruptive, violent, or terroristic. Campus unrest has taken each of these forms. Protest is disruptive when it interferes with the normal activities of the university, or the right of others to carry on their affairs. Obstructive sit-ins, interference with classroom teaching, blockading recruits, and preventing others from speaking or hearing speakers are further examples of disruptive protest.

Violent protest involves physical injury to people ranging from bloodied noses and cracked heads to actual death. It involves the willful destruction of property by vandalism, burning, and bombing.

A small but highly publicized number of student protests can be called terroristic. Terrorism involves the careful planning and deliberate use of violence in a systematic way in order to create an atmosphere of fear to obtain revolutionary political change.

Each manifestation of campus unrest calls for a different response. Peaceful, orderly, and lawful, protest must be protected. Violent and terroristic protest must be dealt with under the law by law enforcement agencies. Disruptive protest is in the first instance the responsibility of the university.

We will return to these distinctions over and over again in this report.

Appendix III

Report of the President's Commission on Campus Unrest (1970), Washington, D.C. To the American People

The crisis on American campuses has no parallel in the history of the nation. This crisis has roots in divisions of American society as deep as any since the Civil War. The divisions are reflected in violent acts and harsh rhetoric, and in the enmity of those Americans who see themselves as occupying opposing camps. Campus unrest reflects and increases a more profound crisis in the nation as a whole.

This crisis has two components: a crisis of violence and a crisis of understanding. We fear new violence and growing enmity.

Crisis of Violence

On the nation's campuses, and in their neighboring communities, the level of violence has been steadily rising. Students have been killed and injured; civil authorities have been killed and injured; bystanders have been killed and injured. Valuable public and private property, and scholarly products have been burned.

Too many Americans have begun to justify violence as a means of effecting change or safeguarding traditions. Too many have forgotten the values and sense of shared humanity that unite us. Campus violence reflects this national condition.

Much of the nation is so polarized that on many campuses a major domestic conflict or an unpopular initiative in foreign policy could trigger further violence protest and, in its wake, counterviolence and repression.

The Constitution protects the freedom of all citizens to dissent and to engage in nonviolent protest. Dissent is a healthy sign of freedom and a protection against stagnation. But the right to dissent is not the right to resort to violence.

Equally, to respond to peaceful protest with repression and brutal tactics is dangerously unwise. It makes extremists of moderates, deepens the divisions in the nation, and increases the chances that future protest will be violent.

We believe it urgent that Americans of all convictions draw back from the brink. We must recognize even our bitter opponents as fellow Americans with rights upon which we cannot morally or legally encroach and as fellow human beings whom we must not club, stone, shoot, or bomb.

We utterly condemn violence. Students who bomb and burn are criminals. Police and National Guardsmen who needlessly shoot or assault students are criminals. All who applaud these criminal acts share in their evil. We must declare a national cease-fire.

There can be no more "trashing," no more rock throwing, no more arson, no more bombing by protestors. No grievance, philosophy, or political idea can justify the destruction and killing we have witnessed. There can be no sanctuary or immunity from prosecution on the campus. If our society is to survive, criminal acts by students must be treated as such wherever they occur and whatever their purpose.

Crimes committed by one do not justify crimes committed by another. We condemn brutality and excessive force by officers and troops called to maintain order. The use of force by police is sometimes necessary and legal, but every unnecessary resort to violence is wrong, criminal, and feeds the hostility of the disaffected.

Our universities as centers of free inquiry are particularly vulnerable to violence. We condemn those groups which are openly seeking to destroy them.

We especially condemn bombing and political terrorism. The full resources of society must be employed to bring to justice those who commit terroristic acts. Anyone who aids or protects terrorists, on or off campus, must share the moral and legal responsibilities for the crimes they commit.

We find ominous and shocking reports that students are laying in supplies of weapons, and that others are preparing to take the law into their hands against protestors and minorities they dislike. There can be no place in our society for vigilantes, night riders, or militants who would bring destruction and death upon their opponents. No one serves the law by breaking it.

Violence must stop because it is wrong. It destroys human life and the products of human effort. It undermines the foundations of a just social order. No progress is possible in a society where lawlessness prevails.

Violence must stop because the sounds of violence drown out all words of reason. When students and officials resort to force and violence, no one can hear and the nation is denied a vital call to conscience. It must stop because no nation will long tolerate violence without repression. History offers grim proof that repression once started is almost impossible to contain.

Crisis of Understanding

Campus protest has been focused on three major questions: war, racial injustice, and the university itself.

The first issue is the unfulfilled promise of full justice and dignity for blacks and other minorities. Blacks, like many others of different races and ethnic origins, are demanding today that the pledges of the Declaration of Independence and the Emancipation proclamation be fulfilled now. Full social justice and dignity—an end to racism, in all its human, social, and cultural forms—is a central demand of today's students, black, brown, and white.

A great majority of students and a majority of their elders oppose the Indochina war. Many believe it entirely immoral. And if the war is wrong, students insist, then so are all policies and practices that support it, from the draft to military research, from ROTC to recruiting for defense industry. This opposition has led to an ever-widening wave of student protests.

A third target of student protest is the shortcomings of the American university. The goals, values, administration, and curriculum have been sharply criticized by many students. Students complain that their studies are irrelevant to the social problems that concern them. They want to shape their own personal and common lives, but find the university restrictive. They seek a community of companions and scholars, but find an impersonal multiversity. And they denounce the university's relationship to the war and to discriminatory racial practices.

Behind the student protest on these issues and the crisis of violence to which they have contributed lies the more basic crisis of understanding.

Americans have never shared a single culture, a single philosophy, or a single religion. But in most periods in our history, we have shared many common values, common sympathies, and a common dedication to a system of government which protects our diversity.

We are now in grave danger of losing what is common among us through growing intolerance of opposing views on issues and of diversity itself.

A "new" culture is emerging primarily among students. Membership is often manifested by differences in dress and lifestyle. Most of its members have high ideals and great fears. They stress the need for humanity, equality, and the sacredness of life. They fear that nuclear war will make them the last generation in history. They see their elders as entrapped by materialism and competition, and prisoners of outdated social forms. They believe their own country has lost its sense of human purpose. They see the Indochina war as an onslaught by a technological giant upon the peasant people of a small, harmless, and backward nation. The war is seen as draining resources from the urgent needs of social and racial justice. They argue that we are the first nation with sufficient resources to create not only decent lives for some, but a decent society for all and that we are failing to do so. They feel they must remake America in its own image.

But among the members of this new student culture, there is a growing lack of tolerance, a growing insistence that their own views must govern, an impatience with the slow procedures of liberal democracy, a growing denial of the humanity and goodwill of those who urge patience and restraint, and particularly of those whose duty it is to enforce the law. A small number of students have turned to violence; an increasing number, not terrorists themselves, would not turn even arsonists and bombers over to law enforcement officials.

At the same time, many Americans have reacted to this emerging culture with an intolerance of their own. They reject not only that which is impatient, unrestrained, and intolerant in the new culture of the young, but even that which is good. Worse, they reject the individual members of the student culture themselves. Distinctive dress alone is enough to draw insult and abuse. Increasing numbers of citizens believe that students who dissent or protest, even those who protest peacefully, deserve to be treated harshly. Some even say that when dissenters are killed, they have brought death upon themselves. Less and less do students and the larger community seek to understand or respect the viewpoint and motivations of the other.

If this trend continues, if this crisis of understanding endures, the very survival of the nation will be threatened. A nation driven to use the weapons of war upon its youth is a nation on the edge of chaos. A nation that has lost the allegiance of part of its youth is a nation that has lost part of its future. A nation whose young have become intolerant of diversity, intolerant of the rest of its citizenry, and intolerant of all traditional values simply because they are traditional, has no generation worthy or capable of assuming leadership in the years to come.

We urgently call for reconciliation. Tolerance and understanding on all sides must reemerge from the fundamental decency of Americans, from our shared aspirations as Americans, from our traditional tolerance of diversity, and from our common humanity. We must regain our compassion for one another and our mutual respect.

There is a deep continuity between all Americans, young and old, a continuity that is being obscured in our growing polarization. Most dissenting youth are striving toward the ultimate values and dreams of their elders and their forefathers. In all Americans there has always been latent respect for the idealism of the young. The whole object of a free government is to allow the nation to redefine its purposes in the light of new needs without sacrificing the accumulated wisdom of its living traditions. We cannot do this without each other.

Despite the differences among us, powerful values and sympathies unite us. The very motto of our nation calls for both unity and diversity: from many, one. Out of our divisions, we must now recreate understanding and respect for those different from ourselves.

Appendix III

Violence must end.

Understanding must be renewed.

All Americans must come to see each other not as symbols or stereotypes but as human beings.

Reconciliation must begin.

We share the impatience of those who call for change. We believe there is still time and opportunity to achieve change. We believe we can still fulfill our shared national commitment to peace, justice, decency, equality, and the celebration of human life.

We must start. All of us.

Our recommendations are directed toward this end.

Appendix IV

Report of the President's Commission on Campus Unrest (1970), Washington, D.C. Major Recommendations

Far more important than the particular recommendations of this Commission are the underlying themes that are common to all:

Most student protestors are neither violent nor extremist. But a small minority of politically extreme students and faculty members and a small group of dedicated agitators are bent on destruction of the university through violence in order to gain their own political ends. Perpetrators of violence must be identified, removed from the university as swiftly as possible, and prosecuted vigorously by the appropriate agencies of law enforcement.

Dissent and peaceful protest are a valued part of this nation's way of governing itself. Violence and disorder are the antithesis of democratic processes and cannot be tolerated either on the nation's campuses or anywhere else.

The roots of student activism lie in unresolved conflicts in our national life, but the many defects of the universities have also fueled campus unrest.

Universities have not adequately prepared themselves to respond to disruption. They have been without suitable plans, rules, or sanctions. Some administrators and faculty members have responded irresolutely. Frequently, announced sanctions have not been applied. Even more frequently, the lack of appropriate organization within the university has rendered its response ineffective. The university's own house must be placed in order.

Too many students have acted irresponsibly and even dangerously in pursuing their stated goals and expressing their dissent. Too many law enforcement officers have responded with unwarranted harshness and force in seeking to control disorder. Actions—and inactions—of government at all levels have contributed to campus unrest. The words of some political leaders have helped to inflame it. Law enforcement officers have too often reacted ineptly or overreacted. At times their response has degenerated into uncontrolled violence.

The nation has been slow to resolve the issues of war and race, which exacerbate divisions within American society and which have contributed to the escalation of student protest and disorder.

All of us must act to prevent violence, to create understanding, and to reduce the bitterness and hostility that divide both the campus and the country. We must establish respect for the processes of law and tolerance for the exercise of dissent on our campuses and in the nation.

We advance our recommendations not as cure-alls, but as rational and responsive steps that should be taken. We summarize here our major recommendations, addressed to those who have the power to carry them out.

A. For the President

We urge that the president exercise his reconciling moral leadership as the first step to prevent violence and create understanding. It is imperative that the president bring us together before more lives are lost and more property destroyed and more universities disrupted.

We recommend that the president seek to convince public officials and protestors alike that divisive and insulting rhetoric is dangerous. In the current political campaign and throughout the years ahead, the president should insist that no one play irresponsible politics with the issue of "campus unrest."

We recommend that the president take the lead in explaining to the American people the underlying causes of campus unrest and the urgency of our present situation. We recommend that he articulate and emphasize those values all Americans hold in common. At the same time we urge him to point out the importance of diversity and coexistence to the nation's health.

To this end, nothing is more important than an end to the war in Indochina. Disaffected students see the war as a symbol of moral crisis in the nation which, in their eyes, deprives even law of its legitimacy. Their dramatic reaction to the Cambodian invasion was a measure of the intensity of their moral recoil.

We urge the president to renew the national commitment to full social justice, and to be aware of increasing charges of repression. We recommend that he take steps to see to it that the words and deeds of government do not encourage belief in those charges.

We recommend that the president lend his personal support and assistance to American universities to accomplish the changes and reforms suggested in this report.

We recommend that the president take steps to assure that he be continuously informed of the views of students and blacks, important constituencies in this nation.

We recommend that the president call a series of national meetings designed to foster understanding among those who are now divided. He should meet with the governors of the states, with university leaders, with law enforcement officers, and with black and student leaders. Each participant in these meetings should be urged to bring with him practical suggestions for restoring trust and responsibility among those whom he represents, and commit himself to continue this process of national reconciliation in frequent meetings throughout the school year.

B. For Government

We strongly urge public officials at all levels of government to recognize that their public statements can either heal or divide. Harsh and bitter rhetoric can set citizen against citizen, exacerbate tension, and encourage violence.

Just as the president must offer reconciling leadership to reunite the nation, so all government officials—at all levels—must work to bring our hostile factions together.

Like the president, the governors of the states should hold meetings and develop contacts throughout the school year to further the cause of reconciliation. Like the president, other federal, state, and local officials must be sensitive to the charge of repression and fashion their words and deeds in a manner designed to refute it.

We urge state and local officials to make plans for handling campus disorders in full cooperation with one another and with the universities. We urge the states to establish guidelines setting forth more precisely the circumstances that justify ordering the guard to intervene in a campus disorder.

We recommend that the federal government review all its current policies affecting students and universities to assure that neither the policies nor administration of them threatens the independence or quality of American higher education. At the same time government should increase its financial support of higher education.

We urge public officials to reject demands that entire universities be punished because of the ideas or excesses of some members, and to honor their responsibility to help preserve academic freedom.

We recommend that the Department of Defense establish alternatives to ROTC so that officer education is available to students whose universities choose to terminate on-campus ROTC programs.

We recommend greatly increased financial aid for black colleges and universities. All agencies of government that support such institutions should massively increase their grants to enable these colleges to overcome past shortcomings.

We support the continuing efforts of formerly all-white universities to recruit black, Mexican-American, Puerto Rican, and other minority students, and we urge that adequate government-sponsored student aid be made available to them. We recommend that in the process of becoming more representative of the society at large, universities make the adjustments necessary to permit those from minority backgrounds to take maximum advantage of their university experience.

Bombing and arson pose an increasing threat to lives and property on campus. We urge prompt enactment of strict controls over the sale, transfer, and possession of explosive materials. Such statutes are needed at both the federal and state levels.

C. For Law Enforcement

We have deep sympathy for peace officers—local and state police, National Guardsmen, and campus security officers—who must deal with all types of campus disorder. Much depends on their judgment, courage, and professionalism.

We commend those thousands of law enforcement officers who have endured taunts and assaults without reacting violently, and whose careful conduct has prevented violence and saved lives.

At the same time, we recognize that there have been dangerous and sometimes fatal instances of unnecessary harshness and illegal violence by law enforcement officers.

We therefore urge that peace officers be trained and equipped to deal with campus disorders, firmly, justly, and humanely. They must avoid both uncontrolled and excessive response.

Too frequently, local police forces have been undermanned, improperly equipped, poorly trained, and unprepared for campus disturbances. We therefore urge police forces, especially those in smaller communities, to improve their capacity to respond to civil disorders.

We recommend the development of joint contingency plans among law enforcement agencies. They should specify which law enforcement official is to be in command when several forces are operating together.

Sending civil authorities on to a college campus as if for war—armed only to kill—has brought tragedy in the past. If this practice is not changed, tragedy will come again. Shoulder weapons (except for tear gas launchers) are very rarely needed on the college campus; they should not be used except as emergency equipment in the face of sniper fire or armed resistance justifying them.

We recommend that National Guardsmen receive much more training in controlling civil disturbances. During the last three years, the guard has played almost no role in Southeast Asia, but has been called to intervene in civil disorders at home more than two hundred times.

We urge that the National Guard be issued special protection equipment appropriate for use in controlling civil disorders. We urge that it have sufficient tactical capability and nonlethal weaponry so that it will use deadly force only as the absolute last resort.

D. For the University

Every university must improve its capability for responding effectively to disorder. Students, faculty, and trustees must support these efforts. Universities must pull themselves together.

The university should be an open forum where speakers

of every point of view can be heard. The area of permitted speech and conduct should be at least as broad as that protected by the First Amendment.

The university should promulgate a code making clear the limits of permissible conduct and announce in advance what measures it is willing to employ in response to impermissible conduct. It should strengthen its disciplinary process. It should assess the capabilities of its security force and determine what role, if any, that force should play in responding to disorder.

When criminal violence occurs on the campus, university officials should promptly call for the assistance of law enforcement agencies.

When faced with disruptive but nonviolent conduct, the university should be prepared to respond initially with internal measures. It must clearly understand the options available to it and be prepared to move from one to another if it is reasonably obvious that an earlier tactic has failed.

Faculty members who engage in or lead disruptive conduct have no place in the university community.

The university, and particularly the faculty, must recognize that the expansion of higher education and the emergence of the new youth culture have changed the makeup and concerns of today's student population. The university should adapt itself to these new conditions. We urge that the university make its teaching programs, degree structure, and transfer and leave policies more flexible and more varied in order to enhance the quality and voluntariness of university study.

We call upon all members of the university to reaffirm that the proper functions of the university are teaching and learning, research and scholarship. An academic community best serves itself, the country, and every principle to which it is devoted by concentrating on these tasks.

Academic institutions must be free—free from outside interference, and free from internal intimidation. Far too many people who should know better—both within university communities and outside them—have forgotten this first principle of academic freedom. The pursuit of knowledge cannot continue without the free exchange of ideas.

Obviously, all members of the academic community, as individuals, should be free to participate actively in whatever campaigns or causes they choose. But universities as institutions must remain politically neutral, except in those rare cases in which their own integrity, educational purpose, or preservation is at stake.

One of the most valid criticisms of many universities is that their faculties have become so involved in outside research that their commitment to teaching seems compromised. We urge universities and faculty members to reduce their outside service commitments. We recognize that alternative sources of university funding will have to be developed to take the place of the money attached to these outside commitments. Realistically, this will mean more unrestricted government aid to higher education.

Large universities should take steps to decentralize or reorganize to make possible a more human scale.

University governance systems should be reformed to increase participation of students and faculty in the formulation of university policies that affect them. But universities cannot be run on a one-man, one-vote basis with participation of all members on all issues.

Universities must become true communities whose members share a sense of respect, tolerance, and responsibility for one another.

E. For Students

Students must accept the responsibility of presenting their ideas in a reasonable and persuasive manner. They must recognize that they are citizens of a nation which was founded on tolerance and diversity, and they must become more understanding of those with whom they differ.

Students must protect the right of all speakers to be heard even when they disagree with the point of view expressed. Heckling speakers is not only bad manners but is inimical to all the values that a university stands for.

Students must face the fact that giving moral support to those who are planning violent action is morally despicable.

Students should be reminded that language that offends

will seldom persuade. Their words have sometimes seemed as offensive to many Americans as the words of some public officials have been to them.

Students should not expect their own views, even if held with great moral intensity, automatically and immediately to determine national policy. The rhetorical commitment to democracy by students must be matched by an awareness of the central role of majority rule in a democratic society, and by an equal commitment to techniques of persuasion within the political process.

The Commission has been impressed and moved by the idealism and commitment of American youth. But this extraordinary commitment brings with it extraordinary obligations: to learn from our nation's past experience, to recognize the humanity of those with whom they disagree, and to maintain their respect for the rule of law. The fight for change and justice is the good fight; to drop out or strike out at the first sign of failure is to insure that change will never come.

This Commission is only too aware of America's shortcomings. Yet we are also a nation of enduring strength. Millions of Americans—generations past and present—have given their vision, their energy, and their patient labor to make us a more just nation and a more humane people. We who seek to change America today build on their accomplishments and enjoy the freedoms they won for us. It is a considerable inheritance; we must not squander or destroy it.

About the Author

Philip Caputo is the author of the *New York Times* bestseller *A Rumor of War* and numerous novels. He won the Pulitzer Prize in 1972 as part of an investigative team for the *Chicago Tribune*, and his coverage of his experience as a captive of Palestinian guerrillas won him the Overseas Press Club's George Polk Citation. He lives in Norwalk, Connecticut, with his wife, Leslie Ware.